Teaching Music to Students with Autism

Teaching Music to Students with Autism

Alice M. Hammel

Ryan M. Hourigan

OXFORD
UNIVERSITY PRESS

OXFORD
UNIVERSITY PRESS

Oxford University Press is a department of the University of Oxford.
It furthers the University's objective of excellence in research, scholarship,
and education by publishing worldwide.

Oxford   New York
Auckland   Cape Town   Dar es Salaam   Hong Kong   Karachi
Kuala Lumpur   Madrid   Melbourne   Mexico City   Nairobi
New Delhi   Shanghai   Taipei Toronto

With offices in
Argentina   Austria   Brazil   Chile   Czech Republic   France   Greece
Guatemala   Hungary   Italy   Japan   Poland   Portugal   Singapore
South Korea   Switzerland   Thailand   Turkey   Ukraine   Vietnam

Oxford is a registered trademark of Oxford University Press
in the UK and certain other countries.

Published in the United States of America by
Oxford University Press
198 Madison Avenue, New York, NY 10016

Library of Congress Cataloging-in-Publication Data
Hammel, Alice, author.
Teaching music to students with autism / Alice M. Hammel, Ryan M. Hourigan.
pages cm
Includes bibliographical references and index.
ISBN 978–0–19–985677–0 (hardcover : alk. paper) — ISBN 978–0–19–985676–3 (pbk. : alk.
paper)   1. Children with autism spectrum disorders—Education—Music.   2. Autistic children—
Education—Music.   3. Special education—Music.   4. Music—Instruction and study.   I. Hourigan,
Ryan M., author.   II. Title.
ML3920.H27 2013
616.89'1654—dc23
2012051118

This text is dedicated to the countless music educators who work with students on the autism spectrum every day, and to the wonderful, inspiring children with autism that we have had the pleasure of making music with over many years. As always, our families provide the support and space needed to write. Furthermore, we are grateful to our spouses and children for their belief in the importance of our endeavors.

Bruce, Amy, Hannah, Hollie, Joshua, and Andrew—we are your biggest fans!

This text is dedicated to the countless music educators who work with students on the autism spectrum every day, and to the wonderful, inspiring children with autism that we have had the pleasure of making music with over many years. As always, our families provide the support and space needed to write. Furthermore, we are grateful to our spouses and children for their belief in the importance of our endeavors.

Bruce, Amy, Hannah, Hollie, Joshua, and Andrew—we are your biggest fans!

CONTENTS

Foreword by Marilyn Friend   xi
Preface   xv
Acknowledgments   xix

1. What Is Autism Spectrum Disorder? An Explanation of the
   Diagnosis   *1*
   Autism Spectrum Disorders: Diagnostic Information   2
   Change in Diagnostic Criteria   3
   Characteristics or Features of Autism Spectrum Disorder   3
   How Do I Know I Am Teaching a Student with Autism Spectrum
      Disorder?   4
   Early Intervention   5
   Typical Interventions and Treatment Models   6
   Applied Behavior Analysis and Discrete Trial Training   7
   Treatment and Education of Autistic and Related Communication-
      Handicapped Children (TEACCH) Curriculum   8
   DIR/Floortime   9
   Cognitive Coaching   11
   Social Stories   12
   Conclusion   13
   References   13
   Discussion Questions   14
2. A Team Approach to Teaching Music to Students with Autism
   Spectrum Disorder   15
   Learning about Your Student(s) with Autism Spectrum
      Disorder   16
   Learning about Other Educators, Therapists, and Professionals in
      the District   18
   Building Relationships with Parents   20
   Building Relationships with Other Staff Members   22
   Administrative Support   22
   Participation in Meetings   23

Understanding the Least Restrictive Environment and a Student
   with Autism Spectrum Disorder   24
Student Profile Revisited   26
Questions for the IEP/504 Meeting   28
Conclusion   28
References   29
Discussion Questions and Suggested Activities   30

3. Understanding Communication and Students with Autism Spectrum
   Disorder   31
   Unique Communication Characteristics of Persons with
      Autism   32
   Complications with Eye Gaze or Eye Contact   32
   Eye Contact and Theory of Mind   33
   Inattentiveness and Eye Contact   34
   Echolalia   35
   Joint Attention   37
   Reciprocation   38
   Receptive and Expressive Language Skills   40
   Receptive Language   40
   Expressive Language Development (Cause and Effect)   42
   Strategies for Music Educators in Expressive and Receptive
      Language   43
   Steps to Affective Communication with Students with Autism in the
      Music Classroom   43
   Step 1: Establish Eye Contact   43
   Step 2: Encourage Joint Attention   44
   Step 3: Encourage Reciprocation   44
   Augmentative and Alternative Communication for Students with
      Autism   45
   Communication Interruptions (a Failure to Communicate)   47
   Social Stories   48
   Conclusion   50
   References   50
   Discussion Questions   51

4. Understanding Cognition and Students with Autism Spectrum
   Disorder   52
   Theory of Mind and Cognition   55
   Weak Central Coherence   57
   Strategies for Assisting with Central Coherence Challenges   57
   Executive Function   59
   Joint Attention (as It Relates to Cognition)   63

Musical Cognition, Perception, and Response in Students with
 Autism   65
Conclusion   67
References   67
Discussion Questions   68

5. Classroom Behavior and Students with Autism   69
 Child Behavior Development and Students with Autism   70
 Understanding Applied Behavior Analysis and Discrete Trial
  Training   72
 Outbursts, Meltdowns, and Other Disruptions   73
 The Antecedent   74
 The Behavior   74
 The Consequence   75
 Odd or Repetitive Behavior   75
 Behavior and Communication   76
 Schedule, Routine, and the Link with Behavior   77
 Creating a Behavior Plan for a Student with Autism   81
 Social Skills and Behavior   83
 Related Medical Issues and Behavior   83
 Conclusion: Assessment of Behavior (Taking Data for the
  IEP)   84
 References   85
 Discussion Questions   86

6. Understanding the Socialization of Students with Autism Spectrum
 Disorder   87
 The Fundamentals of Social Development and Children with
  Autism   89
 Gaze/Eye Contact, Joint Attention, and Socialization   89
 Extending Eye Contact and Joint Attention in the Music
  Classroom   90
 Social Speech and Social Play   91
 Social Speech and Social Play in the Music Classroom   94
 Affective Development   95
 Affective Development in the Music Classroom   95
 Imitation   96
 Peer Relationships and Social Interaction   97
 Peer Relationships and Social Interaction in the Music
  Classroom   98
 Reverse Inclusion   99
 Conclusion   100
 References   101
 Discussion Questions   102

7. Autism, Sensory Dysfunction, and Music Education   *103*
    Tactile Challenges in the Music Classroom   *105*
    Vestibular and Proprioceptive Challenges in the Music
        Classroom   *106*
    Visual Dysfunction   *108*
    Auditory Sensitivity and Dysfunction   *109*
    Sensory Motor/Motor Planning/Dyspraxia   *110*
    Self-Stimulating Sensory Behaviors   *111*
    Sensory Breaks (Conclusion)   *113*
    References   *113*
    Discussion Questions   *114*
8. Advocacy for Students with Autism in Music Education   *115*
    Fostering Relationships with All Stakeholders   *116*
        Parents   *116*
        Special Educators   *120*
        Special Education Administrators   *122*
        Classroom Teachers   *122*
    Conditions for Music Learning for Students with Autism   *123*
        Learning Environment   *123*
        One-on-One Support   *124*
        Multiple Ways to Demonstrate Knowledge   *124*
        Teacher Qualities That Must Exist in Music Classrooms   *125*
    Local Community Not-for-Profit Organizations   *126*
    Public "Informances" Including Students with Autism   *126*
    Student Support and Awareness Groups   *126*
    Conclusion   *128*
    References   *129*
    Discussion Questions   *130*
9. Classroom and Ensemble Snapshots of Teaching Music to Students
    with Autism   *131*
    Classroom-based Examples of Teaching Music to Students with
        Autism   *132*
    Performance-based Examples of Teaching Music to Students with
        Austism   *135*
    Conclusion   *145*
10. Resources for Music Teachers   *147*
    Internet Resources   *147*
    Print Resources for Music Educators and Music Teacher
        Educators   *154*

About the Authors   *159*
Index   *163*

In July 2012, the Kennedy Center for the Performing Arts Education Department, Very Special Arts and Accessibility Office hosted a two-day invitational meeting in Washington, DC, called Examining the Intersection of Arts Education and Special Education: A National Forum. In the midst of spirited discussion, insightful analyses, and refreshingly innovative brainstorming about bringing the arts and arts education to children and youth with disabilities, I met and was immediately impressed by Alice Hammel and Ryan Hourigan, two eminently accomplished music professionals, educators, and scholars. And so, when they asked me to write a foreword for their book on teaching music to students with autism, I was delighted to make a small contribution to their effort.

Drs. Hammel and Hourigan have accomplished so much in *Teaching Music to Students with Autism* that it is difficult to know which elements to highlight in this brief foreword. First, they have placed a much-needed spotlight on the importance for students with autism (or any special need, for that matter) to have true access to the music instruction available in schools. In this day and age, when so many education conversations focus on improving outcomes and reducing the achievement gap between typical students and students with disabilities, it is crucial to recognize that there is more to life than traditional academic achievement and that music should be part of students' school experience. But the authors, clearly recognizing that just wishing for this access will not cause it to happen, carefully provide the specific strategies and techniques that can make music inclusiveness a reality—from teaching young children a hello song to facilitating the participation of students with autism in high school chorus. Further, they specifically focus on all those other topics beyond music instruction that demand attention, including facilitating peer interactions, communicating with students who may have significant language problems, and responding to unusual or challenging student behaviors.

Equally important, Drs. Hammel and Hourigan emphasize throughout the book the role of collaboration. They do this in a balanced way—they accentuate the contribution that music teachers can make to the understanding of students with autism spectrum disorder and reaching these students through music. At the same time, they stress the need for music teachers to seek out the expertise of their colleagues who are special educators; related service providers, such as speech-language therapists; and administrators for information about students, for materials and other resources, and for technical assistance. Especially significant is the authors' careful attention to partnerships with parents and how such collaboration can enhance student growth.

I am captivated by the explanations Drs. Hammel and Hourigan provide to music teachers for instructing students with autism. They outline approaches that communicate the need for patience and persistence (teaching a student first where to place his thumb on his instrument and not worrying about where to place fingers until that step is mastered), and they do this with examples across all grade levels and different types of music experiences. What they demonstrate is that teaching students with autism requires innovation and diligence, and that this hard work can have a tremendous payoff in student learning and enjoyment. They focus on identifying what students can do and on helping them learn to do more rather than emphasize what students cannot do. The message for music teachers is reflective of Temple Grandin's words: "*I cannot emphasize enough the importance of a good teacher.*"

Another striking dimension of this book is the way Drs. Hammel and Hourigan tackle background material on special education and the field of autism. They give their readers enough detail that they will understand the meanings of terms that might be heard in meetings and methods and programs that might be discussed, but not so much minutiae that a music teacher without background in this area would feel overwhelmed. That is, they introduce terms such as *least restrictive environment* and describe approaches such as *discrete trial training* and Picture Exchange Communication System (PECS), providing just the essential concepts, often illustrated with examples of real students. Given the contemporary professional and popular press tsunami of information about autism, their skillful selection of essential concepts is a noteworthy achievement.

Still other aspects of *Teaching Music to Students with Autism* make it a valuable resource for practitioners. For example, the book is filled with specific examples—of students, of situations, of teachers' experiences, of strategies and approaches. These examples are realistic (yes, even meltdowns are respectfully addressed). Sometimes there is a happy ending, but occasionally the situations cannot be resolved. The vignettes about students are especially powerful as they draw the reader into the situation and compel reflection and problem solving. This book should be required reading in music teacher professional-preparation programs.

My own career has been characterized by my passion for ensuring that students with disabilities are educated in ways that enable them to truly reach their potential, especially through the collaborative efforts of professionals and parents. In fact, that was the reason I was in attendance at the Kennedy Center forum where I met Drs. Hammel and Hourigan. What a fortuitous encounter! It's clear they are kindred spirits, passionate about making music instruction accessible to students with autism spectrum disorder. Their enthusiasm comes through clearly on each page, and you will find yourself saying, "I'm sure I could do that. Yes, that would work." I hope you enjoy your reading journey—I most certainly did!

Marilyn Friend, PhD
Past President, Council for Exceptional Children
Professor Emerita
Department of Specialized Education Services
The University of North Carolina at Greensboro

PREFACE

According to the Autism Society of America (2013), 1 out of 88 children born in the United States are diagnosed with autism spectrum disorder (http://www.autism-society.org). Over the past decade, many music teachers have seen an increase in the number of students with autism included in their music classrooms. Statistics suggest that inevitably, every music teacher will eventually teach a student with autism spectrum disorder.

Teaching Music to Students with Autism is a comprehensive guide for music teachers who struggle to accommodate and modify lessons and curricula for students with autism spectrum disorder. The information in this text has been coalesced from years of teaching students with autism, travel to over 30 states speaking and working with music teachers, and research conducted in the field of students with autism and other students with special needs in music. This book is designed for inservice music educators, preservice music educators, and music teacher educators and is designed as a comprehensive manual, reference, and advocacy guide that introduces those in the field of music education to best practices when teaching music to students with autism. This book is an extension of *Teaching Music to Students with Special Needs: A Label free Approach* (2011) and delineates the teaching and learning relationship with students with autism through five domains (communication, cognition, behavior, sensory, physical). The socialization category is added to the current discussion because many students with autism struggle in this area, and socialization challenges are considered to be a hallmark of the diagnosis of autism.

We have organized the book with diagnosis and policy information in the first two chapters, followed by individual chapters that focus on individual areas of concern for most children with autism spectrum disorder (communication, cognition, behavior, socialization, and sensory needs). The last two chapters are designed to allow the reader to generalize real-life teaching situations into their own music classrooms, followed by a detailed resource chapter.

Chapter 1 is designed to explain the diagnosis of autism spectrum disorder and how unique characteristics associated with this disorder manifest themselves in the music classroom. We also provide a brief explanation of various treatment and intervention models to understand the various expectations that students with autism have across their curricula. It is hoped that music teachers will benefit by understanding and generalizing some of these expectations to provide consistency in the music classroom for students with autism.

Chapter 2 focuses on building relationships with other faculty, service providers, administrators, students, and parents as they work together to provide a team approach to the teaching and learning environment of children with autism spectrum disorder. This includes working to provide the least restrictive environment for a child with autism and understanding how to collect and report information about students with autism at IEP (Individualized Education Program) meetings. This chapter also provides information regarding different service providers and their roles in providing services for students with autism. Music teachers will benefit from knowing how other professionals in their buildings work with and teach students with autism. This will allow for consistent and effective interventions and strategies for all involved in a child's school day.

Without communication between music teacher and student, there is little chance for learning in the music classroom. Chapter 3 emphasizes the need for enhanced communicative support for students with autism including the unique communication characteristics that children with autism use to learn in the music classroom. This chapter includes Augmentative and Alternative Communication (AAC) strategies as well as other techniques including social stories to assist in communicating with students on the autism spectrum.

Chapter 4 accentuates the different ways children with autism think. Topics include theory of mind, central coherence, and executive function all with the focus on how a student with autism perceives, processes, and learns musical concepts. Music teachers will benefit from understanding why certain abstract musical concepts and activities are difficult, and how to strengthen a student's ability to grasp higher-order musical ideas. In addition, suggestions are provided to enhance the experience of higher-functioning students with autism.

Behavior is often a concern for music teachers who teach students with autism. Chapter 5 offers explanations regarding why certain behaviors exist and persist with students who have autism and how to collaborate with other members of the faculty, parents, and other students to promote positive behavior in the music classroom. In addition, chapter 5 includes examples of tested individualized behavior plans that can be implemented in the music classroom or across the curriculum for consistency of expectations.

Behavior is often linked with a student's ability to socialize with his peers. If a child demonstrates behaviors that are inconsistent with those of his peers, he may lose the ability to sustain long-lasting relationships. Many music teachers understand that the school music experience is enhanced if it can be experienced within a social learning environment. Chapter 6 in this text provides inclusion and socialization strategies specifically for the music student with autism and his peers. These techniques include extending joint attention, modeling, affective development, and peer interaction.

One of the pillars of autism is sensory dysfunction. Many students with autism, while trying to learn music, also are struggling with tactile (touch), vestibular and proprioceptive (balance), visual, auditory, and sensory motor challenges. Chapter 7 provides detailed explanations regarding ways the abovementioned sensory challenges affect a child with autism, and how music teachers can accommodate these needs.

From our many visits to classrooms and conversations with music teachers, service providers, parents, and professionals, we felt the need to offer a chapter with a specific focus on advocacy and children with autism. Many students are inappropriately placed in classrooms (including music classrooms) that are not in accordance with their least restrictive environment or a Free Appropriate Public Education (FAPE). Chapter 8 provides ideas regarding fostering relationships with stakeholders in offering the most appropriate learning environment for students with autism.

Finally, chapters 9 and 10 are intended to be resource guides for music teachers currently in classrooms (pre-K-12). Chapter 9 provides real-life examples written by music teachers who teach students with autism in public schools in various regions of the United States. The intent is to offer readers insight, wisdom, and ideas from music teachers who have a wealth of experience teaching music to students with autism. Chapter 10 is the result of an exhaustive search for resources—websites, books, journal articles, apps, and other media—on the topic of teaching music to students with autism. This book also has a companion website where these resources will be periodically updated and new resources added.

There is an increasing advocacy effort designed to provide access for all, inclusion whenever possible, and true social justice within music education classrooms. With the increasing diversity of populations of students taught in public schools, the philosophy, teaching practices, and paradigm presented in this text readily transfer to the ideas that center on what a meaningful and culturally, socially, socioeconomically, and disability responsive music classroom can mean to our students, whether they are diagnosed with autism or not. We invite you to join this conversation through the reading of this text and by seeking to provide this education to students who have autism.

ACKNOWLEDGMENTS

We would like to thank Craig Standish, Kelly Fisher, Jim Shouldice, Beth O'Riordan Leah Sullenbarger, Joy Anderson, Berta Hickox, and Susan Harvey for their contributions to this book. In addition, we would like to thank Shannan Hibbard for her extensive work on Chapter 10. We are grateful to Norm Hirschy, our editor, who has been consistently supportive of our efforts and a champion for our cause. Lastly, we would like to thank our family, friends, and colleagues who have supported the completion of this book.

Teaching Music to Students with Autism

CHAPTER 1

What Is Autism Spectrum Disorder?

An Explanation of the Diagnosis

CHAPTER OVERVIEW

To truly understand a child with autism, music educators must understand the diagnosis and features of autism. This chapter includes the following topics:

- Diagnostic information
- Characteristics and features of autism
- Typical interventions and treatment models

The word autism comes from the Greek word *autos* meaning "self." Leo Kanner first described childhood autism in 1943 as affecting children in the area of "social dysfunction" and "unusual responses" (Carter, Davis, Klin & Volkmar, 2005, 312). Since the middle of the twentieth century there has been much research into the diagnosis of autism spectrum disorder (ASD). This chapter is designed to give music teachers a broad understanding of ASD, how it is diagnosed and how students with autism receive treatment in and out of public school. Later chapters offer music teaching techniques based on research and best practice. We also examine ways to develop partnerships with special educators and parents to provide the best music-learning environment for students with autism. However, before we can examine these best practices, we will explore techniques used to treat and educate students with autism. Careful thought and review of current strategies allow our music classrooms to be aligned with expectations, understandings, and philosophies that exist across the curriculum.

AUTISM SPECTRUM DISORDERS: DIAGNOSTIC INFORMATION

Autism is a complex neurological disorder that medically falls within the category of pervasive developmental disorders (PDDs). The *American Psychological Association Diagnostic and Statistical Manual* (*DSM-IV-TR*) lists several disorders that fall under the PDD spectrum. Autism is one of these disorders. Others include pervasive developmental disorder not otherwise specified (PDD-NOS), Asperger syndrome, Rett syndrome, and childhood disintegrative disorder. Specifically, according to the Autism Society of America, "autism is a complex developmental disability that typically appears during the first three years of life and affects a person's ability to communicate and interact with others. Autism is defined by a certain set of behaviors and is a 'spectrum disorder' that affects individuals differently and to varying degrees" (Autism Society of America, 2013).

Symptoms of ASD usually occur within the first three years of life (typically around 18 months). These symptoms include lack of eye contact, lack of babbling or cooing by 12 months, no gesturing (pointing, waving, grasping) by 12 months, no language by 16 months, no two-word phrases on his or her own by 24 months, and loss of any language or social skill at any age (Autism Society of America, 2013). When a teacher or parent states, "Mark is on the spectrum," this person is referring to the fact that Mark's diagnosis is one of the disorders mentioned above. Figure 1.1 gives a brief description of each disorder on the PDD spectrum.

Autistic Spectrum Disorder: Autism is a general term used to describe a group of complex developmental brain disorders known as Pervasive developmental disorders (PDD).

Pervasive Development Disorder Not Otherwise Specified: Pervasive developmental disorder not otherwise specified, or PDD-NOS, is a condition on the spectrum that describes those who exhibit some, but not all, of the symptoms associated with classic autism. This can include difficulty socializing with others, repetitive behaviors, and heightened sensitivities to certain stimuli. (Autismspeaks.org)

Asperger's syndrome: This syndrome affects the ability of a person to socialize and communicate with others. Persons with Asperger's Syndrome are often considered high functioning according to the spectrum.

Childhood Disintegrative Disorder (a.k.a. Heller's syndrome): Characterized by normal development up to age 2 to 4 years then a gradual loss of communication and social skills.

Rett Syndrome: The National Institute of Neurological Disorders and Stroke says children who have Rett syndrome can have problems walking and speaking, may exhibit repetitive behaviors (usually involving their hands) and may also have mental retardation. The condition presents itself in four stages, from "early onset," which may begin when children are as young as six months, to "late motor deterioration," which can render them nearly immobilized.

Figure 1.1
Pervasive Developmental Disorders

CHANGE IN DIAGNOSTIC CRITERIA

An examination of the diagnosis of autism cannot be complete without including the current discussion regarding Asperger syndrome and autism. The new *DSM-V* lists Asperger syndrome under the same category without a separate distinction. The following statement appears on the American Psychological Association's website:

> Autism spectrum disorder is a new DSM-5 name that reflects a scientific consensus that four previously separate disorders are actually a single condition with different levels of symptom severity in two core domains. ASD now encompasses the previous DSM-IV autistic disorder (autism), Asperger's disorder, childhood disintegrative disorder, and pervasive developmental disorder not otherwise specified. ASD is characterized by 1) deficits in social communication and social interaction and 2) restricted repetitive behaviors, interests, and activities (RRBs). Because both components are required for diagnosis of ASD, social communication disorder is diagnosed if no RRBs are present.
>
> (American Psychiatric Association, 2013)

For the purposes of this book, we will use Asperger syndrome and other labels that previously appeared in the *DSM IV*. We realize, however, that like attention deficit disorder (ADD), these labels may eventually fade from the vernacular. Also, in order to maintain the flow of the conversation and to use terms that are familiar to practicing teachers, we will also use the terms "autism" and "ASD" to refer to students who are diagnosed with autism spectrum disorder.

Characteristics or Features of Autism Spectrum Disorder

Persons within the autism spectrum exhibit impairments (not limited to) in the following areas: delays in social and communication skills and restrictive, repetitive behaviors, interests or activities. Many students with autism will display a limited repertoire of activities and interests. Another, similar feature is the lack of joint attention and an inability to read facial expressions and body language. These features appear with shocking consistency among all children and adults with autism and are truly hallmarks of the diagnosis. Throughout this book, we will define, describe, and explore these primary features of autism.

It is important to understand that ASD is a life-long disorder that has a wide variance in behavioral and neurological characteristics. All persons with autism manifest these impairments in various ways, and in varying degrees, throughout their lives. This is another use of the term "spectrum."

CAUTIONARY CONSIDERATIONS

- Do not ask parents or caregivers if their child has autism. Many parents will still be working with providers to determine the exact diagnosis or working through their own life changes as a result of a diagnosis. If possible, focus on the positive attributes a child brings to your classroom.

When a teacher or professional refers to a person being "on the spectrum," he or she may also be referring to the degree to which a person exhibits these characteristics.

Four times as many boys (1 out of 70) are diagnosed with autism as girls (Autism Speaks, 2013). Many persons with autism test below average on intelligence quotient (IQ) measures, although some persons with autism do demonstrate average to above-average intelligence. Approximately 30% of those with autism do not develop functional speech skills into adulthood (Ozonoff et al., 2003). Therefore, many adults with autism often have significant cognitive capabilities; however, they lack the means to develop those capabilities because of communication barriers.

In recent years, the media has often commented on the increased incidence of autism. Many ascribe the increase to a more finely defined, yet broadly inclusive, set of diagnostic tools. Others contend more children are being born with autism than ever before and that the increase in prevalence is not related to the diagnostic procedures. Researchers are not certain of the cause of autism. Genetics may play a role in determining whether a child will be diagnosed with autism. Researchers have also not completely discarded the role the environment may have in the development of autism (Siegel, 2003).

These discussions will, no doubt, continue. For the purpose of this book, the premise is that both arguments have merit; however, we focus on one main goal: to provide information and strategies that will improve the quality of education students with autism receive in the music classroom. The diagnostic discussions can be left to biomedical researchers.

HOW DO I KNOW I AM TEACHING A STUDENT WITH AUTISM SPECTRUM DISORDER?

According to federal law, parents are not required to disclose a child's diagnosis to all teachers. However, parents and students often choose to disclose this information. Some local and schoolwide policies allow teachers access to this information and, depending on the state, the diagnosis may be included in your accommodation or Individualized Education Program (IEP) information. As always, seek out a special education professional first with questions regarding a student in the music classroom who may have autism. It is because of this label-free trend in special education that many music educators consider the five domains of learning: communication, cognition, behavioral/emotional, sensorial, and physical (Hammel & Hourigan, 2011), rather than rely on specific labels and etiology attached to those generic labels.

EARLY INTERVENTION

As mentioned earlier, autism is a spectrum disorder. Because of this, each person with autism displays different behaviors, and will possess varying degrees of skills and deficits. This makes diagnosis, therapy options, and educational planning difficult for families and professionals. The most successful plan is to start with treatment and therapy options as early as possible.

Physicians and educators are becoming increasingly aware of various signs of autism, and the availability of early intervention services is increasing (NEC, 2001). The professionals who are qualified to provide early intervention include physicians, special educators, general educators, psychologists, speech pathologists, music therapists, and developmental physical/occupational therapists.

Early intervention, consistent treatment, and therapy plans are important in the lives of young children with autism. The longer a family or professional team waits to begin intervention, the less likely it is that the student will progress. There are many philosophical and practical considerations in choosing a treatment plan or set of plans. Some plans work very well for some children. It is worth bearing in mind that autism is a very individual disorder and there is no one method for addressing it. There are a few well-known methods of treatment and intervention that also apply to an inclusion or self-contained music classroom.

Many music educators teach students at the prekindergarten or preschool level. Young students with autism may be involved in intense early-intervention programs during this time and may have limited access to music programs. When they do have access, they may be fatigued and unable to participate as fully or as often as other students in the class who do not spend as much time in therapeutic or intervention settings. Some young children (ages one to three years) may spend many hours in intensified therapy. In addition, if any of the characteristics mentioned earlier

---

CAUTIONARY CONSIDERATIONS

- Do not force a young child with autism to participate in an early-childhood or early-elementary music class. This child may need time and space in the music room before feeling comfortable enough to participate.

---

manifest themselves in the classroom, it is advisable to seek a licensed professional (e.g., a special educator or occupational or speech therapist) to express specific concerns. Music educators are not necessarily autism experts. There are trained professionals in the school community, such as social workers, special education administrators, and therapists, who are charged with the responsibility of contacting parents and scheduling necessary steps involved in providing a diagnosis or service. They are the first contact in regard to these questions.

TYPICAL INTERVENTIONS AND TREATMENT MODELS

Because autism manifests differently in each individual, when an educator has taught *one* student with autism, she has learned about only *one* student with autism. The educator may then proceed to learn about a second student with autism and find that each student enters the music classroom with a wide array of needs. As part of that learning process, it is critical that music teachers understand the life of a typical child with autism during the time that child is not in the music classroom.

Depending on when or if a child is diagnosed, students with autism may be involved in one or more therapies and interventions mentioned in this chapter. Therefore, when trying to engage students with autism, it is useful to understand the ways therapists and other providers communicate and engage with the student. The information provided below is an overview of various models used to treat and educate students with autism. Knowledge of these models allows music educators to look deeper (if needed) if they see something similar used to educate a child with autism. It is easier for a student on the spectrum to learn within a consistent paradigm or learning environment. For example, if students are used to earning rewards in their other behaviorist-style classrooms and therapy sessions, music teachers may find it easier to structure lessons in a similar way. As always, music educators are encouraged to consult with the special education area in their school when implementing these ideas in the music classroom. The education of a student with autism is most effective when a team of teachers including special education, therapy, and music educators are consistent in their expectations, approaches, and reward systems.

Applied Behavior Analysis and Discrete Trial Training

Behavior analysis focuses on the principles that explain how learning takes place in people. Professionals who study behaviors in persons with autism create discrete sets of microbehaviors and determine whether or not a behavior is conducive to the process of learning (Autism Speaks, 2013). Often, positive reinforcement is used to reward desired learning behaviors, while other behaviors are not reinforced or are ignored altogether. Simply put, behaviors that are appropriate and move a person toward a learning goal are reinforced. This is often referred to as "behavioral conditioning."

Applied Behavior Analysis (ABA) through Discrete Trial Training (DTT) is the science of behavioral conditioning in a therapeutic or classroom situation. Tasks, information, skills, and sequences can be taught by creating small steps (discrete trials) or pieces from a larger set of behaviors. Teachers and therapists who use ABA in their work provide many opportunities for a student to respond behaviorally. Each step and positive response by the student is rewarded. An appropriate reward is any item or form of positive reinforcement that causes the student to increase the amount and frequency of a desired behavior.

Dr. Ivar Lovaas at the University of California, Los Angeles, a leading researcher on autism and founder of the Lovaas Institute (http://www.lovaas.com) created this method in the late 1960s. Each skill within a set of skills is taught as a discrete and separate task. A very basic way of explaining the heart of this method is that a child learns that he must do something to get something in return. For many children with autism, this is the beginning of their experience with ABA. By increasing the amount, time, distance, and complexity of tasks, students can begin to learn sequences, as the teacher fades into the background and decreases the frequency of rewards. A caution about using a reward system is to observe for satiation: if a reward is used too often, or in too great a quantity, a student may lose interest in that particular reward. A second caution is to be sure the reward chosen truly functions as a reward for the student.

A modified ABA or DTT model can be used successfully in the music classroom. Any behavior can be taught, and with time, repetition, and patience, students with autism can be shown the skills and behaviors used in music. Many music teachers begin by combining sign language with auditory directions. Some students begin their first new behavior by learning to walk into the music classroom. Upon successfully entering the classroom, the student may then be taught how and where to sit, when to stand, and what the procedures are for beginning class (Sobol, 2008). A music educator can work with students this way in a classroom environment; however, it is more effective to use ABA when there is an aide or another adult in the classroom to provide prompts and rewards. Applied behavior, as it applies to music learning and basic behavior, will be discussed in detail as this text progresses (chapter 5). Verbal Behavior Analysis (VBA) is an extension of ABA and is often used with students on the spectrum. The same principles apply only with language, focusing on teaching a child that using language will get them what they want or need. Specific applications of ABA techniques with classroom behavior will be discussed in chapter 5.

Classroom behavior is an area where ABA techniques can be used with success. Each positive behavior (e.g., raising your hand, taking turns) can be reinforced with a reward (e.g., choice time with drums or with a toy). Behaviors that a music teacher would like to curtail, such as talking out of turn and loud outbursts, can be ignored with the goal that students will realize certain behaviors are rewarded and others are not. Again, specific applications of ABA techniques with classroom behavior are discussed in chapter 5.

Treatment and Education of Autistic and Related Communication-Handicapped Children Curriculum

Dr. Eric Schoppler at the University of North Carolina at Chapel Hill, a noted expert in teaching students with autism, developed the Treatment and Education of Autistic and Related Communication-Handicapped Children (TEACCH) curriculum. The overall goal of TEACCH is to create learning environments for students with autism that are accessible and familiar. Teachers and professionals develop classrooms that specifically complement the strengths, preferences, and interests of students with autism. They then use this environment as the baseline for all educational and social goals. Often, these environments are very visual and extremely structured with predictable routines that are oriented toward the specific needs of the students. The structured setting includes a "rule" or way of doing for each separate skill throughout the day. Picture or word schedules are always available and each student has a specific task to complete every minute of the day. Students are allowed more time to complete tasks and can begin to learn to redirect their off-task behaviors themselves rather than repeatedly being given an ABA prompt. Picture Exchange Communication Systems (PECS) are used often in TEACCH classrooms as students learn to ask or show to respond or indicate a request. A detailed explanation of PECS is examined in chapter 3.

TEACCH can work very well in a self-contained music classroom. Music teachers who apply this method will often choose songs, games, and activities that are based on the interests of their students. By creating an environment that is focused on these student interests, music teachers begin from a position that is familiar to the student. This interest can also be strengthened through the use of visuals. These visuals can include puppets, manipulatives, teacher-created cards and videos that demonstrate the desired behaviors and actions for the student. One effective strategy is to take pictures of the individual student participating in each desired activity. The pictures can be laminated and put together to create a book by punching a hole in the pictures and attaching them to a metal ring. This book then becomes the lesson sequence. The student works through the visual lesson sequence using the pictures of himself as prompts. Boardmaker includes many line drawings, which are often easier for a student with autism to interpret as facial expressions because unnecessary information has been removed. Students with autism may choose two or three pictures to indicate a desired activity. The cards are also effective when students wish to communicate that they need a break or to use the restroom.

It is more difficult to adapt PECS to an inclusion classroom without an aide or other adult present. However, students with autism are often able to apply TEACCH strategies from their special education classroom to the music classroom. The use of PECS, a picture schedule, a very well-known and often-repeated set of activities and songs, and a consistent schedule are all excellent strategies to use when teaching music to students with autism. In this way, the strategies effective in a self-contained classroom can be applied to the inclusion classroom with the assistance of an additional adult or fellow student. These teaching techniques will be discussed at length throughout this text.

DIR/Floortime

The Developmental, Individual Difference, Relationship-based (DIR®) Model is a specific framework that helps clinicians, parents, and educators develop a specific intervention program tailored to the unique challenges and strengths of a child with autism (http://www.icdl.com). This intervention plan is based on the child's developmental level and the individual differences of the child. All the therapies and interventions associated with this paradigm are relationship based, meaning that their techniques are based on strengthening a child's ability to initiate and maintain relationships with others.

While at the National Institute of Mental Health, Dr. Stanley Greenspan developed the Floortime model. This model uses the exchange of signals between teacher and student as the basis for learning behaviors and information. It then builds sequences of behaviors in students through a combination of structured trials, relationship-building exercises, and frequent positive reinforcement, often using activities that a child finds uniquely interesting.

Students and teachers engage in joint-attention activities (the teacher and student taking interest in the same item or activity) with the student taking the lead in performing activities. Teachers often find ways to include social and academic goals as part of this play process (Heflin, 2007). For a simple example, a child may be interested in firefighters. The teacher or therapists would begin by allowing a student to play with a fire truck. If the child is verbal, the teacher may ask, "May I have a turn with the fire truck?" thus establishing a turn-taking event. The therapist or teacher may extend this activity by sharing the truck back and forth with the child or going as far as talking about what the fireman would say or do, all to extend the joint interest in playing with the fire truck. These joint-attention activities can be lengthened and often become more sophisticated as the student progresses. Therapists then move through communication and socialization skills, all based on the relationship and interest of the student.

The Floortime approach may not be as easy to transfer to the inclusive music classroom as other approaches. In a self-contained setting, it may also be difficult to create meaningful personal relationships within a group of students. The most useful transfer of this model is that when students are given the option to lead, and a teacher happily follows, a playful and joint-attention activity can result: music. This is an excellent step is developing a relationship that will allow productive music making to take place (Siegel, 2003).

Students with autism also have a tendency to become fully invested in one specific subject or activity. If this subject is something musical, or can be connected to music in some way, the Floortime technique can be used in the music classroom. For example, allow a student who is interested in

CAUTIONARY CONSIDERATIONS

- Do not determine or predetermine the therapy you think best for a particular student. Instead, attempt to incorporate elements of that therapy into the music classroom or ensemble to provide stability and consistency. Remember, unless you are a licensed therapist, you are not able to provide therapy. The information in this section is provided to help you remain consistent in your classroom. Always consult the special education team.

pipe organs to learn everything there is to know about pipe organs. Learning how organs are made, organ composers, places where there are great organs, organ music, and so forth, allows the student to explore this topic based on his interest. An advantage of this technique is that students can work on an individual level and independently. Much of this style of teaching is similar to constructivism. We offer extensive discussion and techniques in our previous book, *Teaching Music to Student with Special Needs: A Label-Free Approach* (2011, 123) as well.

Cognitive Coaching

Coaching is another approach that has been especially effective with students who have autism and are functioning fairly well in school and home settings (National Research Council, 2001). This cognitive approach addresses the underlying causes and motives for behaviors. Students are asked why they engage in a particular behavior and are coached to try more successful ways of achieving their goals. Making students aware of how their behavior affects them and others is a primary goal of this method. Through daily or weekly cognitive work, students are encouraged to think before acting and to make choices that are consistent with their overall academic and social well-being.

In a music classroom, coaching can work very well. Students with autism need frequent reminders, models, and reteaching. A student who receives even a few minutes of cognitive coaching at the end of a music class or ensemble rehearsal can begin to develop connections between the discussion and his behaviors (academic and social) in the next class. Coaching can also involve viewing videos of the student in class as the teacher talks about what is happening and what could perhaps happen in the future.

Students with autism often have great difficulty understanding how their behavior appears to and affects others. Through cognitive coaching, students can begin to see patterns of cause and effect in their daily interactions. For example, an eighth-grade choral student, Danyele, may initially be unable to discern why her choral director is disappointed in her. The teacher called Danyele's mother and expressed concern because Danyele had been very rude to another student in class. During class, Danyele told the other student that her shirt was ugly and that she thought it was funny that the student had received a lower grade on a music theory test. This disrupted class, caused the other student to cry, and other choral students to loudly chide Danyele for yet another set of poor choices. Through daily cognitive coaching, Danyele can begin to see the results of making careful choices in her words and actions.

This approach takes time, preferably daily coaching, and positive results can require several months or years of work. Once a student is able to cognitively comprehend these relationships, her behavior may be modified for a lifetime. Cognitive coaching is not a "quick fix"; however, it has potential for great success in the life of a student with autism.

Social Stories

Because students with autism have impairments in social and communication skills, they often need repeated rehearsal to engage in academic and social settings with others. Creating a social story can be effective in alleviating anxiety and increasing success for students with autism (Gray, 2000). A social story is very similar to a task analysis. Each step in the process of an event or procedure is depicted visually, and a scripted story is created and rehearsed. These stories are sometimes laminated and made into a book that students can use as they engage in the activity described in the story. We discuss music applications of social stories throughout this book.

A transfer to the music classroom may include a way to appropriately play a game. In first grade, many students sing and play the game Apple Tree. Jimmy may have great difficulty following the rules of a game and may cry if he is out during that game. A social story can demonstrate (visual/ aural) the steps in playing the game, the rules, and a story of a boy named Jimmy who can sing and follow the rules. In the story, Jimmy has fun following the steps in the game, and does not cry if he is out and does not win the game. There are several examples of social stories for use in the music classroom throughout the book. They can be used for emotional, behavior, social, and academic needs.

There are many other treatment models in use for students on the autism spectrum. The selected models we have mentioned represent a few that are among the most common. Music educators are encouraged to inquire with

---

CAUTIONARY CONSIDERATIONS

- Do not engage a student with autism in a cognitive coaching situation for a longer period of time than the student is eagerly and fully participating.

the special education team about types of therapies and treatments utilized to gain a deeper understanding of a student. This will assist the music teacher and the student in music learning.

CONCLUSION

Music educators often seek to improve their effectiveness with students who have special needs. When the music teacher has information regarding the diagnosis and treatment models, and an ability to converse with other school professionals, it can be a joy to work with students who have autism. This basic overview introduced tools that are helpful when the music teacher is conversing with classroom teachers, special educators, and professionals to create the best learning environment for students with autism. This team approach will be addressed in subsequent chapters to include ways to advocate for music programs and all students, those with and without special needs.

REFERENCES

The American Psychiatric Association (2013). *Highlights of Changes from* DSV-IV *to* DSM-V. American Psychiatric Association website. Retrieved February 19, 2013, www.psychiatry.org.

Autism Society of America (2013). Autism Society website. Retrieved February 18, 2013, http://www.autism-society.org.

Autism Speaks. (2013). Autism Speaks website. Retreived February 18, 2013, http://www.autismspeaks.org.

Carter, A. S., Davis, N. O., Klin, A., and Volkmar (2005). Social development in autism. In F. R. Volkmar, R. Paul, A. Klin, & D. Cohen (eds.), *Handbook of autism and pervasive developmental disorders.* Hokoken, NJ: John Wiley & Sons, 312–334.

Gray, C. (2000). *The new social story book.* Arlington, TX: Future Horizons.

Hammel, A., & Hourigan R. M. (2011). *Teaching music to students with special needs: A label-free approach.* New York: Oxford University Press.

Heflin, J. L., & Alaimo, D. F. (2007). *Students with autism spectrum disorders.* Upper Saddle River, NJ: Pearson Education.

Lopez-Duran, N. (2010). *Autism and Asperger's in the DSM-V: Thoughts on clinical utility.*

National Research Council (2001). *Educating children with autism.* Division of Behavioral and Social Sciences and Education. Washington, DC: National Academy Press.

Ozonoff, S., Rogers, S., & Hendren, R. (2003). *Autism spectrum disorders: A research review for practitioners.* American Psychiatric Publishing: Washington DC.

Siegel, B. (2003). *Helping children with autism learn.* New York: Oxford University Press.

Sobol, E. S. (2008). *An attitude and approach for teaching music to special learners* (2nd ed.). Reston, VA: MENC: The National Association for Music Education/Rowman & Littlefield Education.

DISCUSSION QUESTIONS

1. Do you know anyone close to you who has been diagnosed with autism spectrum disorder? Was it a child? If so, how did the parents determine that something was unique about their child?
2. How can knowing the treatment and therapies your students participate in on a daily or weekly basis inform your teaching?
3. What are some effective strategies when becoming a member of the special education team?

CHAPTER 2

A Team Approach to Teaching Music to Students with Autism Spectrum Disorder

---

CHAPTER OVERVIEW

Successful inclusion of students with autism spectrum disorder into the music classroom depends heavily on the positive relationships that are formed among general education teachers, music educators, special educators, administrators, paraprofessionals, parents, and students. This chapter includes the following topics:

1. Learning about students with autism spectrum disorder
2. Establishing relationships with other special educators, therapists, and administrators
3. Establishing relationships with other staff members
4. Participating in meetings (including IEP meetings)
5. Understanding the least restrictive environment and students with autism
6. Making use of student profiles as data

Some teachers are inherently team oriented. For others, the idea of working as a team can seem complicated and intimidating. Music teachers are often the only educators in a building that work in their area of concentration. As a result, music educators are not necessarily accustomed to collaborating on a daily or weekly basis with other professionals, especially special educators and therapists. Music teachers may have been placed on committees or teams with other teachers; however, establishing a meaningful place within those teams can be questionable. For those fortunate music educators who find working on a team to be integral and instructive to their teaching, adapting the team approach when working with students who have autism will be a natural step.

This chapter offers communication strategies that are successful when collaborating with other members of the team within the special education area. These strategies assist music educators in gathering and presenting information as decisions are made regarding the least restrictive environment (LRE) for a student with autism. Some music educators are unaware of roles assigned to other professionals in the building and have not actively fostered relationships with parents. A goal of this chapter is to provide essential information regarding the role of a music educator within the special education team. Strategies in this chapter are useful for music teachers working with students with autism spectrum disorder as well as those with other types of special needs.

LEARNING ABOUT YOUR STUDENT(S) WITH AUTISM SPECTRUM DISORDER

The first step toward becoming an effective team member is to collect data that will be valued by other team members and stakeholders. Strategies for collecting data will be discussed throughout this text as they pertain to certain attributes of including students with ASD. By gathering information about a student, the process is made more efficient and practical. Naturally, this begins by becoming more familiar with the student. Reviewing IEP and Section 504 paperwork as well as other school files will provide essential background information. While reading this information, take note of any acronyms that are unfamiliar. Also, make lists or an outline of specific personal, communication, emotional, academic, sensory, and social needs the student may have, as well as her academic goals in other areas.

The next step is to take some time to observe the student in another classroom. This may require setting aside some planning time or eating lunch while observing. During these observations, look for similar issues that may occur in your classroom, such as communication strategies, behavioral concerns, teaching strategies, or other concerns. For example, if a music teacher perceives that sound sensitivity may be an issue for the student, he can look for accommodations that are made for that student regarding this sensory issue in a physical education or math class.

To start the lesson planning and data-collection process, it is very useful to write a profile about the student being studied. It may be in an outline, list, or paragraph format. It generally includes information about the student at home, at school, and in any other recurring activities. This profile also describes the student's areas of strength as well as his or her challenges in different learning environments. It lists any specific classroom adaptations and accommodations. Finally, it is appropriate for the music teacher to transfer the accommodations listed in the paperwork and observation notes to music classroom lesson plans. This can be a difficult transfer to make and is often the point at which music educators begin to ask for further input from other team members.

Here is an example of a student profile:

Susan has autism spectrum disorder and is in an auditioned ninth-grade concert chorus. This is her first year in chorus after an unsuccessful attempt at violin. She auditioned for the group at the end of the eighth grade. The audition piece was the Star-Spangled Banner. *The director was very impressed with Susan's voice and immediately accepted her into the first soprano section, without knowledge of her autism. Susan reads at the second-grade level. She has an excellent sense of pitch and a lovely singing voice. She is very motivated to learn and loves chorus. Susan also sings in church choir, where her director teaches primarily by rote.*

Susan is extremely popular with her peers. Her peers know she has difficulty with social cues, reading, and communicating with others when they are not discussing an area of personal interest to her. Her parents pay for private tutoring and therapy out of school; however, she still struggles in school.

During the first week of school, things go remarkably well for Susan in chorus. They are practicing for the first assembly, where they will sing the school song, the Star-Spangled Banner, *and an easy arrangement of* This Land Is Your Land.

In week two, the new music and music folders are created and the director asks the students to get them from the music cabinet. The folders are full of new music and are filed according to the student's last name. Susan cannot find her folder, and becomes extremely frustrated and anxious about these new changes and expectations. This puzzles the teacher who has still not received any information about Susan being a student with special needs or, specifically, autism. By the end of that rehearsal, the choral director has made a note to see the guidance counselor during lunch break because she knows Susan will need assistance.

At this point, the teacher needs to access IEP summaries that assess Susan's present level of functioning. She also needs to meet with the special education teacher and Susan's parents to get a better idea of her abilities, disabilities, and some direction regarding accommodations for Susan in choir. The choir director may not be told, and may not know, that Susan's specific special need is that she is on the autism spectrum. The director can, however, evaluate the areas of need Susan has in choir and can plan to meet those needs through accommodations and adaptations. By working as a member of a team, the choir director will be responding to Susan's communication, behavioral/emotional, sensory, cognitive, and physical needs.

Possible solutions to help Susan include some of the following:

1. *Making an audio file of the music—preferably before the music is introduced in class. It will be best if this only includes the soprano line. Later, it may be helpful to include all parts on the file.*
2. *Adapting music theory work according to her IEP needs and reading level.*
3. *Allowing Susan to use a highlighter (erasable) on her music so that she can more easily see her vocal line.*
4. *Creating social stories about rehearsals to allow Susan to participate as freely as possible with her peers during class.*
5. *Establishing a signal between Susan and the teacher that will alert the teacher when Susan becomes overwhelmed or anxious during class.*

During study hall, perhaps Susan can practice by listening to her music. Her special education teacher should be supplied with copies of all the songs Susan is going to sing. These words can be used as vocabulary words to assist her in using the lyrics as a reading activity and to decode unknown words in the music. Furthermore, any written communication regarding field trips, competitions, fundraisers, concerts, and so forth, should be reviewed aurally with Susan so she will understand the importance of taking this information home to her parents.

LEARNING ABOUT OTHER EDUCATORS, THERAPISTS, AND PROFESSIONALS IN THE DISTRICT

Every professional in a school district has her own individual set of skills that are needed to educate a student with autism spectrum disorder. Each specialist also has an area of understanding that can be shared with other professionals. A further part of becoming an effective team member is to identify the other members of the team and to identify their areas of expertise. Each professional in a school has a set of inherent strengths. Identifying and utilizing those strengths is an essential part of team building. In addition, doing this creates a relationship that allows teachers to freely share information and strategies across the curriculum. Addressing this aspect of team building can begin before the start of the school year, through casual conversation before and after meetings, when passing each other in the hallways, and while preparing classrooms.

Some music educators have had great success holding "open houses" toward the end of the week before the start of school. An inexpensive purchase of cookies and lemonade, and an open invitation to come by the music classroom can bring groups of teachers who are hungry by mid-afternoon. Once colleagues meet in the music classroom, it is an easy pivot to talk about student needs and to ask for advice regarding general classroom happenings and procedures. Visiting teachers in their classrooms, perhaps with the same offer of cookies, can also be a good opportunity to initiate conversations about student needs.

There are also technological ways to keep in touch with members of the team. For example, setting up a Facebook, Google, or Yahoo group focused on a student (with parental permission) can be effective. Teachers can set the parameters to generate an automatic e-mail notification to the entire group when someone from the team posts a question or concern. Parents can also be part of these groups, as they are important stakeholders in the process.

The first contact for a music teacher should be the case manager. This person is often the teacher or co-teacher of record if the student is in an elementary school. In a middle school or a high school, there is usually a similar special education professional charged with coordinating accommodations and modifications for the student. Each student with autism will typically have one professional who is charged with overseeing the IEP or 504 documents. In most cases, this is the same person. Being aware of the professional who manages the paperwork for a specific student can be helpful when you are seeking specific, current, and accurate information as well as when identifying other, nonclassroom professionals (e.g., therapists and social workers).

Besides the case manager, there are several types of therapists who are usually employed by a school district to implement IEP/504 goals. These include speech, occupational, physical, music/art, and behavior therapists. Figure 2.1 lists the different types of therapy providers and a description of how they may work with a student with autism. Therapists are often connected to a specific classroom and visit a class to collect data on a child or to see how well a student is functioning in a classroom. They are valuable colleagues who can provide adaptation and accommodation ideas for music teachers. Each of these therapists provides assessments and individualized assistance to students with autism. These therapies may occur as often as every day.

Once the specific expertise of teachers and therapists becomes evident, it is easier to begin asking them for advice and seeking strategies. Any teacher may be asked to assist in a brainstorming process. If the teacher is not actively part of a student's team, discussing the situation using generalities rather than specific names and descriptors is more appropriate because of confidentiality issues. A very effective strategy is to approach teachers and therapists, acknowledge their specific areas of strength (classroom management plans, adaptive technology, relationships with parents, changes to law and practice, speech, etc.), and to ask their assistance based on their expertise. All teachers appreciate acknowledgment of their strengths, and

Speech Therapist: An awareness of speech therapy goals can lead a music educator to adapt language expectations (receptive and expressive) and patterns of speech used in the classroom. It is also helpful to utilize the sounds (consonants, phonemes, etc.) used in therapy with a student in the classroom.

Occupational Therapist: Students with autism often require amelioration of gross and fine motor deficits. They may also receive therapy related to sensory (hypo and hyper) needs the student with autism may have. Use of the same sensory items as well as adaptation of materials from physical therapy to music to meet the current functioning levels of students with autism can be very effective.

Physical Therapist: Students with autism often have difficulty with motor planning and physical tasks. Adaptive equipment and materials assist students with autism as they encounter an inclusion or self-contained classroom. Physical therapists are often aware of a variety of resources that can be effective in the music classroom.

Art/Music Therapist: Art and Music therapists apply arts-related therapy for students with autism. They are often excellent partners with music teachers when considering the present level of functioning and specific goals for students with autism. The use of art and music to can be powerful in the life of a student with autism as they provide unique avenues for receptive and expressive language as well as opportunities for growth in communication, cognition, behavioral/emotional, sensory, and physical areas.

Behavior Therapist: Behavior therapists often craft and implement plans specific to a student with autism. These plans may be adapted for use in an inclusion or self-contained setting. Behavior therapists are also often excellent partners when brainstorming behavior plans for students with special needs.

Figure 2.1
Explanation of the Roles of District-Employed Therapists

doing this will most assuredly increase rapport. Asking others for assistance is a strong initial step toward increasing success with students who have autism. By developing these relationships, the team that works with students becomes much stronger.

BUILDING RELATIONSHIPS WITH PARENTS

Facilitating open communication with the parents and guardians of students with autism can cause concern for some music educators. Teachers may not know how to approach a parent of a child with autism in an appropriate manner. Classroom and special education teachers have more frequent and regular contact with parents, whereas music educators sometimes only see their students once a week. Because of this, music educators do not always have the same amount or quality of opportunities for opening and establishing lines of communication with parents.

An effective strategy is to call the home of a student to share a positive story or accomplishment in the music classroom with the parents. Many parents of students with autism are accustomed to frequent, and often negative, communication from the school system. Seeing the school identified on the caller ID feature of the phone can be unnerving to parents, as they may expect another negative interaction regarding their child. Opening the phone call with a positive story can make the parent begin to feel comfortable talking with the music educator. A further effective strategy is to acknowledge that the parent is an expert about her child and to ask whether the parent has any strategies or ideas that would help the music educator be a better teacher. Being asked for advice can be empowering for the parent of a child with autism.

Try to focus the conversation on specific events or behaviors, and on teaching and learning in the classroom. *Do not introduce the topic of the specific diagnosis.* The parent may not feel comfortable talking directly about his child's autism diagnosis with a teacher (and it is unprofessional and possibly against the law in some states to cite the disability label before the parent discloses it). It may take time for parents to develop trust and to become more open about their child's challenges. Keep the focus on the classroom. Ultimately, having a specific diagnostic label is less important than honoring the personhood of the student with autism and developing strategies to improve the way that student functions in a music classroom or ensemble.

When an event such as a meltdown or an incident related to a sensory issue occurs, parents can often provide the best answer regarding how to correct the problem. If a good rapport exists with the family, this will make it easier to understand challenges and ask for support. If there is an area of noncompliance with the IEP, parents can often be an influence toward change, especially if they are informed about special education law and their child's rights. For example, if a student is not being provided with the necessary aides and services during music time, the parents may be able to request these items on behalf of the music educator.

CAUTIONARY CONSIDERATIONS

- Do not assume you know more about a student with autism spectrum disorder than the parent of the student. Just because you are a trained professional does not mean that you know the ins and outs of caring for a child. Remember, parents spend many hours with their children. A teacher can easily cause tension in a relationship by talking down to a parent.

BUILDING RELATIONSHIPS WITH OTHER
STAFF MEMBERS

In each school, there are other staff members who work with students with autism on a regular basis. The school guidance counselors and nurse; cafeteria, office, and media-center staff; bus drivers; and aides all hold important roles in the daily school life of students with autism. Of these staff members, it is often the aides (or paraprofessionals) who spend the most time with the student. Yet in planning discussions and in building team relationships, the paraprofessionals are sometimes not considered a part of the team. It is imperative that they be included. It is the paraprofessionals who may spend each day at the side of, or very near, a student with autism. Their input can be priceless.

In addition, the paraprofessional can also act as a necessary conduit for communication among the teacher, student, and parent. For example, many students on the spectrum have trouble articulating their homework to their parents. Paraprofessionals can keep notes of each class and the next day's homework assignment and may be able to provide the parent with an e-mail address or phone number for questions. They are also able to provide specific information regarding rehearsals, performances, or other music opportunities through these communication notebooks.

ADMINISTRATIVE SUPPORT

The support of administration can be critical when the music teacher is working with students who have autism. The most successful music educators develop relationships with their administration based on mutual respect and the frequent sharing of information. It is also effective to be vocal in communicating a wholehearted enthusiasm for teaching students with autism (and all students with special needs). This initial and repeated philosophy is welcome and appreciated by administrative personnel.

Each administration has specific protocol for responding to student behavior. Many students with autism are disciplined differently if their behavioral infraction is a result of their disability (impulse control, lack of cognitive awareness, frustration regarding communication with others). Music educators are not always made aware of these differences, and a close working partnership with administrators can assist, with frequent communication in this area. Administrators can also be reminded of a sincere interest in teaching students with autism through consistent communication that is positive and used to solve issues (rather than complain). Once this relationship is established, administrators may be much more likely to include music educators in these conversations and to allow release time for music educators to participate in IEP and 504 meetings with the team.

PARTICIPATION IN MEETINGS

Several strategies can be used when participating in a first IEP or 504 meeting. The first is to choose a student with autism who is excelling in music and to discuss these strengths and positive behaviors during the IEP meeting. The opportunity to be part of the meeting, to listen to various stakeholders as they share their experiences with the student, and to be ready with positive and encouraging words regarding the student can be a good first experience. Once a music educator is aware of the specifics of a team meeting, it can be much easier to plan for participation in subsequent meetings.

A second strategy is to request to be present at a meeting for a student who is not doing well in music. Of course, it is ideal to have all music educators present for all meetings. In reality, however, the meetings are often scheduled during the time students are attending music or at a time that is convenient for the family, rather than the music teacher. It is sometimes effective to request that the meeting be scheduled when the music teacher is available (or a substitute can be provided in the music classroom) after the teacher has collected data and become a true member of the team through his collaborative efforts. If specific data and narrative information can be utilized as part of this request, the importance of the presence of the music educator can be highlighted and understood.

This request can be made at any time. However, it is most meaningful if the music educator has built relationships in the ways we have discussed. By communicating with all stakeholders in the process of supporting a student with autism (teachers, specialists, therapists, staff, administration, parents), the music educator places himself in a position of strength at the meeting. When the lines of communication, team building, and preparatory groundwork have been laid, it can be much easier to advocate for appropriate placement, supplemental equipment, participation time, and personnel support to create the Free Appropriate Public Education (FAPE) promised to all students with special needs.

If it is impossible to attend the meeting, it can be effective to send the team your written data, notes, a letter citing current levels of functioning in the music classroom, and adapted rubrics that show academic, social, and behavioral progress to assist the team. The most important goal is to become an integral part of the team in whatever ways possible. The success of the student with autism is secured when all stakeholders (team members) participate in a cooperative and collegial effort.

CAUTIONARY CONSIDERATIONS

- Do not assume that everyone on the team is initially comfortable working together. This may take time and team building. When initiating conversations, ask for input or suggestions. This acknowledges that you respect what other team members bring to the table. Do not neglect the potentially valuable input of therapists and service providers in the school and school district. When everyone works as a team, you will find the most success.
- Do not forget that team members are also individuals, each with a unique set of skills. They also may understand your knowledge and background. It may take time for members of the team to become comfortable with each other and what each has to offer. Do not miss opportunities to participate in meetings. E-mails, letters, and notes can be used effectively if the presence of a music educator is not possible at a meeting. This will strengthen your relationship with all the members of the team.
- Paraprofessionals can be the single most important member of the team. They are the conduit between the classroom teachers, special educators, administrators, and parents. They also have a unique understanding of a child's needs. Unfortunately, they are often poorly paid and do not always get the respect that they deserve.
- Do not undervalue the relationship between the administration and the music area. Often support can come when an administrator can see the value of a music education for *all* students.

UNDERSTANDING THE LEAST RESTRICTIVE ENVIRONMENT AND A STUDENT WITH AUTISM SPECTRUM DISORDER

A goal of working with a team is to determine the Least Restrictive Environment (LRE) for a student with autism spectrum disorder. However, some music educators are not well versed in special education and do not understand LRE. In addition, many undergraduate and graduate methods courses, as well as in-service opportunities, provide information regarding inclusion classrooms and ways to accommodate the needs of all students within the inclusion paradigm. While inclusion is an excellent idea for many students, it is not always the LRE for every student. This is important to understand when participating in an IEP meeting.

LRE is defined in federal Public Law 94-241 as:

> To the maximum extent appropriate, students with disabilities...[will be] educated with students who are not disabled, and special classes, separate schooling, or other removal of students with disabilities from the regular educational environment [may

occur] only when the nature of severity of the disability of a child is such that education in regular classes with use of supplementary aids and services cannot be achieved
satisfactorily for that student.

(Turnbull, Huerta, & Stowe, 2006)

The LRE for a student with autism is the environment in which that student learns best cognitively, emotionally, and socially.

When determining the LRE, the team should not just consider a specific classroom; instead they should look at the entire learning environment. When the team begins to generate ideas for the most appropriate setting for a student, they begin by discussing the general classroom (what is generally thought of as the inclusion classroom). If it is determined that the inclusion classroom, even when supplementary aids and services are provided, is not the most appropriate placement, other classroom environments are considered. These environments include self-contained (made up of only students with autism and fewer students) music classroom settings. This topic is covered thoroughly in a previously published resource by the authors (*Teaching Music to Students with Special Needs: A Label-Free Approach*, 2011). While the inclusion classroom is the first placement considered, it is not necessarily the LRE for all students with autism.

Another option is a self-contained music class that meets in the self-contained classroom. In this setting, students are not asked to transition from their classroom to a new, larger, and less familiar classroom for music. A further music option, if available, is to have the student(s) participate in music with a music therapist. Not all school systems have this option; however, when available, it can be the most appropriate LRE for some students with autism.

The music educator is the music expert on the school staff. Because of this expertise, the input provided by music educators is important when discussing an appropriate placement for students with autism. Becoming an integral part of the team secures this role and creates a place for the music educator in the decision-making process. Many schools have options

CAUTIONARY CONSIDERATIONS

- Do not assume the inclusion classroom is always the least restrictive environmnent. Some students with autism function best in a self-contained classroom free of the distractions of an included classroom. Often, these can be opportunities for *reverse inclusion*, where a general education class can join a self-contained classroom for music.

to accommodate the placement of students with autism in an appropriate setting. These decisions are critical for students with autism. They also affect the music education of students without special needs. An involved, informed and present voice in the process will actively create more appropriate music classroom placements for all students in our schools.

STUDENT PROFILE REVISITED

We recommend that a student-profile format be utilized when gathering information regarding a student with autism. The creation of a profile to be used in a team meeting can be an excellent framework, particularly if the music educator is just beginning to formally address the needs of a student through the team paradigm.

The organization of a profile is similar to that of the legal documents amended during meetings, and the information gleaned from all stakeholders can be presented in a logical manner during the meeting. In addition, the creation of adaptations and accommodations based on those written for the general or special education classroom can be extremely valuable in a meeting. When these strategies are included in the IEP or 504 documents, they become legally binding. If the strategies require the use of new or varied personnel or equipment, those are now mandated and the school must provide them. If the music educator can demonstrate the need for a paraprofessional, assistive technology, or adapted musical instruments, those personnel and equipment needs will then be included in the legal documents and will, by law, be available for the student with autism in a music setting. By being prepared for the meeting in this manner, music educators are increasing the possibility that their student (and every student in the classroom) will receive what they need to learn best in music.

Here is another example:

Melany, a fourth grader, has ASD. Her teacher, Mrs. Smith, has noted that Melany reads well, and writes some words and phrases using a computer, but has difficulty talking with her peers. Melany is also able to perform some American Sign Language gestures. Often, when asked a question, Melany does not look directly at Mrs. Smith or the other children and appears to be focused on other subjects. She does not look anyone directly in the eyes, however, as she has become more familiar with her classmates, Melany is able to communicate through a combination of words, gestures, and symbols.

In her core subjects, Melany's ability to successfully work at grade level is dependent upon the requirements of the subject matter. The Child Study Team recommended curricular adaptations that have increased Melany's ability to complete assignments. Her curricular adaptations involve a combination of simplified objectives in math and language arts as well as altered, functional objectives in the areas of school routines, self-help, and communication. Therefore, at some times during the day, Melany works on the same objectives as her classmates, except at a different level. For instance, when her classmates are using the writing process to write a brief book report on the computer, she fulfills this assignment by completing a form developed by the special education teacher.

While Melany feels comfortable with Mrs. Smith and her classmates, she often overreacts negatively to sounds that no one else seems to hear, interrupts conversations, and appears rude. Mrs. Smith has helped her focus on the communication, social, and self-management skills that will enable her to function more independently in her school and community. For example, if the group work continues for longer than Melany is able to effectively participate, she is given permission to use the computer to write a note about her school day for her take-home journal.

Melany sometimes becomes frustrated in class and acts out by screaming or crying. She has difficulty relating with peers and is unable to choose a group, or find a group, easily. The Child Study Team has recommended that Melany take several preventative movement "breaks" to relieve her stress and that when necessary she use the provided opportunities to perform self-calming strategies to lower her frustration level and to help her stay focused.

In music class, Melany is accompanied by an aide who sits with her. Since she is very limited in her communication skills and cannot sing songs with the group, the music teacher assigns Melany to play simple percussion instruments, but is unsure as to how she can more fully integrate Melany into the music activities.

In music class Melany could perhaps:

- provide sign language for songs, or
- provide ostinato accompaniments to songs sung by the class.

It would be good for her to be able to role play or have a simulation of what the music lesson is going to involve before class. As a part of her difference, Melany is a good "rule follower." She will want to know what the academic as well as behavioral rules are. She may enjoy learning about lines and spaces and their names because they are rules.

Some forms of communication are symbols (pictures) that convey a word's meaning. A chart of symbols or pictures can illustrate what is expected of her, for example, pictures of her displaying good behavior in music.

Students with ASD sometimes obsess about things that are of high personal interest to them. Knowing facts, details, and ideas to include in projects is helpful for students who share Melany's needs. Repetitive motions (like the ostinato) are good for helping Melany contribute to the music class and practice self-calming while allowing her to focus on an enjoyable activity. Melany may need to be *assigned to groups and have peer groups built for her during class. She also needs to be allowed movement breaks as often as she and/or the aide feels necessary. These breaks allow her to practice self-calming strategies.*

QUESTIONS FOR THE IEP/504 MEETING

If the music educator is prepared for the meeting in the ways we have described, very few initial questions will be necessary. If that information or time has not been available, there are some important questions that may be brought to the meeting and asked of the stakeholders present. If it is not possible to attend the meeting, these questions may also be presented to the team members in writing.

1. How can music assist this student in building on her strengths and ameliorating her challenges across the curriculum?
2. How do you present/keep a schedule for this student?
3. What multimodal experiences are best received by the student? Are there any active or passive classroom activities that may not be well received by the student?
4. What "triggers" are evident for the student prior to and/or during music?
5. How can the music educator assist in achieving the communication goals for the student?

CONCLUSION

By building support within your school community and team, you can literally set the stage for success. When faculty, staff, and administrative personnel actively communicate regarding the specific needs of students with special needs, the educational experience that results for the student can be more cohesive. A critical step in that process is that all team members share information and work together. A concern in the music classroom can be addressed through these channels. It is often a successful strategy to speak with one faculty member on the team, make a plan, take data, and to schedule a time to discuss the plan. If the plan was successful, fantastic! If not, bringing another therapist, teacher, or staff member into the brainstorming and planning stage can be effective. When all the team members have been consulted and various plans implemented, the student has the best opportunity to be successful. If all individual, or group, plans are unsuccessful, it is entirely within the right of the music educator to call a team meeting. By maintaining communication with the team, it is perfectly natural to then suggest that all members of the team meet together to talk about classroom setting, supplementary aides and services, and additional support to ensure the student's success in the music classroom.

REFERENCES

Hammel, A., & Hourigan R. M. (2011). *Teaching music to students with special needs: A label-free approach.* New York: Oxford University Press.

Turnbull, R., Huerta, N., & Stowe, M. (2006). *The Individuals with Disabilities Education Act as Amended in 2004.* Upper Saddle River, NJ: Pearson Merrill Prentice Hall.

DISCUSSION QUESTIONS AND SUGGESTED ACTIVITIES

1. Script a phone call home to a parent or guardian regarding a student you teach (or have taught or may teach in the future). List the salient points you would discuss (the strengths a student may have) and the questions you would ask (ideas to assist you in becoming a better teacher for their child).
2. Who are the team members who attend an IEP or 504 meeting? How do you plan to make contact with them, and what areas of a student's school experience would involve each of these professionals?

CHAPTER 3

Understanding Communication and Students with Autism Spectrum Disorder

---

CHAPTER OVERVIEW

Communication is one of the considerable challenges faced by children with autism. Before for a child with autism can learn, he must be able to communicate. This chapter includes the following topics:

- Communication traits and characteristics of persons with autism
- Steps to effective communication with students with autism in the music classroom
- Joint attention
- Reciprocation
- Echolalia
- Receptive and expressive language
- Augmentative and alternative communication for students with autism in the music classroom
- Social stories and communication

Communication is "the ability to receive, send, process, and comprehend concepts of verbal, nonverbal, and graphic symbol systems" (Heflin & Alaimo, 2007, 234). Many persons with autism struggle in one or all of these areas (receiving, sending, processing, comprehending). When assessing the communication needs of students with autism, medical professionals also examine language in social interaction and how persons (mostly children) participate in symbolic and imaginative play (Volkmar & Klin, 2005, 21). Because communication and socialization go hand in hand, one cannot be discussed without the other.

Vignette 3.1
ANDREW

Andrew is eight years old and is in Mr. Clancy's music class. It is the first day of school. Andrew comes into class with his paraprofessional (Ms. Johnson). Mr. Clancy starts his lesson with a "hello song." Andrew immediately covers his ears and hides behind Ms. Johnson. Mr. Clancy continues the lesson and sings "what's your name?" to Andrew. Andrew does not look at Mr. Clancy and will not answer him after multiple attempts. Andrew continues to stare at the multicolored geometric designs on the side of the hand drums and is not responding to the day's music lesson.

Mr. Clancy has never had a student with autism in his music class. He feels that he spent the majority of his time focusing on communicating with Andrew and did not attend to the other students in his class. In addition, Mr. Clancy only completed half of his lesson because of extra time spent with Andrew.

Discussion:

What would you do to encourage communication with Andrew?

What strategies would you use on the second day of music class with all students (including Andrew)?

It is important for music teachers to understand the different ways in which students with autism communicate and how disruptions in communication can lead to challenges in the music classroom. This chapter is designed to explain the typical communication challenges teachers face when teaching students with autism and to suggest practical strategies for music teachers when including students with autism in the music classroom.

UNIQUE COMMUNICATION CHARACTERISTICS OF PERSONS WITH AUTISM

Complications with Eye Gaze or Eye Contact

It has been long established that at a very young age, *eye gaze* plays an important role as children learn to communicate. Tiegerman and Primavera (1984) state: "By 3½ months of age, infants' visual-motor systems are fully mature, and they use eye gaze to learn about the relationships between objects, people, and events, as well as to indicate interests and emotions" (p. 22). However, many children with autism do not develop this ability and often do not attempt to make and continue eye contact with other people.

One reason for this behavior is that eye contact can be very confusing for a child who does not accurately perceive the communicative intent of another person through this channel. Research has also shown that some children with autism do not receive the necessary communicative information through eye gaze because of cognition interruptions or language delays (e.g., the child is not able to attach meaning to gestures or inflections made through eye contact). In these cases, the use of eye contact may be limited or absent as it brings no meaning to the child (National Research Council, 2001). Many young children with autism are evaluated for possible hearing loss because of their inability to engage in eye contact. The missed opportunity experienced by a student with autism who is not able to make eye contact cannot be overstated. These opportunities happen thousands of times in a child's early life, thus compounding early communication challenges.

As an example, many children in preschool and Head Start classes experience story time on a regular basis. The opportunity to sit on the rug and look at a book while the teacher reads a story is a hallmark of early childhood memories. For a young child with autism, story time can be meaningless; as he stares at the light streaming in through the window, he misses the entire story about the sounds we make when we eat (crunch, smack, slurp, and chew). The opportunity to make eye contact with his teacher and with fellow students is also lost. In addition, he missed the incidental opportunities to view color through the illustrations, and to learn from the responses of his classmates. Because this child is not able to focus on the story while sitting with his classmates on the rug, he has lost another 10 minutes of academic, social, emotional, and collaborative opportunities. These opportunities occur constantly, and each time segment places a child with autism further behind his peers.

Eye Contact and Theory of Mind

Students with autism may also have deficits in what is described as "theory of mind" (ToM). This is typically referred to as "mindblindness" (Siegel, 2003). ToM can be defined in the following way: "the awareness of how mental states such as memories, beliefs, desires, and how intentions govern the behavior of self and others" (Baron-Cohen, 2000, 3). In other words, people with ASD are sometimes unable to derive meaning from or assign order to events or actions. For example, students with "mindblindness" may not understand the nonverbal cues a teacher gives, such as to pick up instruments during a music class, to be quiet, or to listen. They also may not be able to detect emotion conveyed in a nonverbal communication, such as a music teacher's dissatisfaction or satisfaction with a response.

As a solution, if a teacher wants to offer an instrument to a student with autism, she may hold the instrument close to her eyes and close to the eyes of the student. Once the student looks at the teacher, he can be taught that if the teacher's eyes and face are smiling, the instrument may then be handed to the student. When the teacher's eyes and face are not smiling, the instrument will not be handed to the student. In this way, the student may learn that eye contact brings information about events and items that may be desirable. Because the student may be unable to derive meaning from the instrument activity, she must be taught each step of the activity as a discrete skill. This demonstration of receptive-language ability is powerful and, with practice, can greatly increase communication between student and teacher. In addition, if there are nonverbal cues that are used for classroom management purposes (e.g., the "quiet" cue), these may need to be clearly articulated to the student and rehearsed many times.

Inattentiveness and Eye Contact

Many music educators have had experience with a student who will not make eye contact or who will fixate on something seemingly unrelated to a conversation or lesson. It may be that this student enjoys finding and studying eye-catching objects, such as geometric shapes, from various perspectives. This behavior is common for a person with autism. It is important for music teachers to understand that lack of eye contact may be a signal of something else occurring in the classroom. For example, a student may be choosing not to make eye contact because of his anxiety related to the music activity. It is possible that a student may fixate on some object because looking at it provides sensory input and fulfills his need for self-stimulation or provides sameness or safety because it is an object he has seen before in familiar surroundings. These are some of the possible reasons a student with autism might focus on something that has no relevance to a music lesson.

Students with autism can also experience a delay or cognitive-process interruption, which can directly affect their ability to process incoming information and potentially delay their response to a verbal cue or prompt. For example, if a music educator asks a student with autism to sing a tonal pattern, it may take her extra time to receive, process, and provide a response to that cue. Therefore, it is important for music educators to consult with the special education team to understand the kinds of response challenges a student may have. There is a fine line between waiting too long for a response (making the student feel inadequate) and providing the appropriate wait time for the situation. Participating in conversations with members of the special education team can be particularly helpful when designing interventions and procedures that are similar to those used in other settings.

Students with autism also encounter many people who may or may not require them to establish appropriate eye contact in conversations with them. This can reinforce the student's lack of eye contact. A solution can be as simple as singing "hello" to Johnny whenever you see him. Once contact has been initiated, wait for Johnny to say hello and make eye contact with you. If he says hello without making eye contact, catch his gaze, look him in the eye, and say hello again. Hopefully, after many trials, he will learn that when he greets you (and after more practice, when he greets anyone) it is appropriate to make eye contact.

The same is true in a classroom setting that contains students who are neurotypical. Strongly encourage students to answer questions, provide musical examples, and communicate with peers while using appropriate eye contact. This will encourage use of similar eye contact in future interactions with teachers and peers. Heflin and Alaimo (2007) explain that "deviations in eye gaze may signal problems understanding the world and may negatively affect communication development" (p. 235). Learning to make eye contact is critical to the overall communication development of students with autism. Through appropriate eye contact, a student gains further information and begins to develop a new channel of communication.

Echolalia

Many persons with autism exhibit echolalia. Echolalia is defined as the repetition of the speech of others (Heflin & Alaimo, 2007). Many educators have experienced interactions with a person with autism who continues to repeat a word or phrase over and over again. This phrase may have come from a conversation or, in some instances, from elsewhere, such as a favorite television show. These words or phrases are delivered with the same inflection the person finds unique about the word or phrase. Often these instances can be immediate (e.g., repeating a word just heard) or delayed (e.g., repeating a segment from a television show seen a month ago). Either form is an inherent part of the vernacular of a typical person with autism.

One strategy for working with students who engage in echolalia is similar to that used when a teacher is not achieving appropriate eye contact with an individual who has autism. Echolalia can be a way for students with autism to excuse themselves from engaging with the world around them. Often, it is a form of reverting to their world (their safe, similar, and coherent world) instead of engaging with the music lesson or the music teacher. Therefore, the strategies used to discourage echolalia are the same as those used to develop eye contact.

If a student engages in echolalia, it is necessary for the music teacher to develop a strategy that will break the cycle of the behavior and draw that student into the music lesson. This may require a teacher to ask the student a question and wait for a response to reengage him. Or, the music teacher can remind the student to stay on topic; we are not "talking about Elmo right now—we are learning music." Sometimes, a teacher may require a student to respond to something, anything, to get them to reengage in the lesson.

When teaching a student with autism, the music teacher may experience frustration if he feels that progress is not being made. One way to avoid this is to take data, constantly. A successful strategy is to create a task analysis of discrete behaviors that lead to larger, more complicated behaviors. This task analysis can be in the form of a checklist that communicates each step along the way (see figure 3.1), and it can be powerful information to provide to parents, special education teachers, and other stakeholders who work with that student. The data can show how far a student has progressed during a nine-week (or other) period of time. An example can be having a

---

o Logan is not demonstrating any connection with the class lesson. He is staring at the glockenspiel and does not respond at all when spoken to and does not make eye contact when the teacher stands in front of him and gets very close to his eyes (zone of proximal intent).

o Logan will make eye contact when the teacher gets very close to his eyes and calls his name repeatedly.

o Logan will make eye contact when the teacher gets very close to his eyes and calls his name once.

o Logan will make eye contact when the teacher gets very close to his eyes.

o Logan will make eye contact when the teacher calls his name from a distance of 12 inches.

o Logan will make eye contact when the teacher shows the Picture Exchange Communication System (PECS) cards depicting the three songs.

o Logan will make eye contact with the teacher and then focus on the PECS cards while the teacher sings the names of the three songs.

o Logan will make eye contact with the teacher and then focus on the specific PEC card that matches the name of the song the teacher is singing.

o Logan will make eye contact with the teacher and then move his eyes to match the specific PEC card when two songs are provided as a choice.

o Logan will make eye contact with the teacher and then move his eyes to match the specific PEC card when three songs are provided as a choice.

o Logan will make eye contact with the teacher and then move his eyes to match the specific PEC card that names the song the class is singing.

o Logan will make eye contact with the teacher and then move his eyes to indicate his preference of song for the class to sing.

Figure 3.1
A Task Analysis

student choose a song or activity from three icons created to communicate intent. If the class has been singing and playing Snail Snail, Doggie Doggie, and Lucy Locket to practice their la-sol-mi patterns, the student can be encouraged to choose the song/game for the class (picture icons can be created for each).

Working through a set of behaviors can take a very long time. If each step is delineated, the process becomes more data driven, and the music educator can track and display the student's progress toward a specific goal. This can also serve as a way to reinforce the teacher as she works each class time to improve the eye gaze and eye contact of a student (or students) with autism.

Joint Attention

Part of the development of communication skills includes the way we attend to the interests of others and share in joint attention to objects and activities. This is an integral part of language development (Sigman & Ruskin, 1999). Unfortunately, this is extremely difficult for some people with autism. Students with autism may not be interested in typical objects, events, people, or situations that interest their peers. They also may not have any interest in engaging with other people. Another way to consider "interest" is to consider that students with autism are sometimes unable to receive any information or reinforcing input by engaging in joint attention with another human. Facial expressions, tone of voice, and the every day happenings of a music classroom can have no meaning because meaning has not been attached.

It is through direct and repeated task behaviors that this "interest" can be taught as a student with autism learns what the cues and information from another human have to do with him (similar to the task analysis created in the joint-attention section of this chapter). In addition, when asked about another person's interests, there may be a variety of reasons these students are not able to respond. Strategies discussed to encourage eye contact and joint attention can similarly be taught through adapting and modifying daily conversations, activities, and events in the music classroom.

It is important to attempt to extend joint attention at every opportunity. In music this may mean extending a pattern-echo exercise or continuing a conversation about a composer or a musical interest for as long as possible. An example is a game of "Simon Says" with pitches. A teacher may begin by singing one pitch (sol) and then encouraging the student to sing that pitch to the teacher. The second step would be to sing two pitches (e.g., sol mi) and then to encourage the student to sing those two pitches at the appropriate time. A new set of these discrete skills can be created to track the progress. If the teacher also includes eye contact while singing the increasingly longer passages, two goals can be met—eye contact and joint attention.

The longer a music educator can hold a student with autism's interest, the more that student will learn. Remember that a child learns by engaging with the world, and that the more these activities are rehearsed, the stronger they will be. Joint attention as it pertains to other aspects of autism is discussed again later in the chapter.

Reciprocation

Conversations with students with autism can be difficult. In addition, the ability to reciprocate conversation also impacts further communication development. This is especially true for students who struggle with the elements of communication discussed earlier in this chapter (e.g., joint attention, eye gaze). Engaging a student with autism to converse with a typical set of reciprocations can be rare. Nevertheless, conversation is still an important part of the formative assessment process for music teachers. In the previous section of this chapter we discussed extending joint attention for as long as possible. Reciprocation can be the key to doing this with a student on the autism spectrum. Once a student reciprocates with one appropriate response, the next step is to add to that response. For the sake of discussion, let's use Andrew from the opening vignette as an example. Once Mrs. Clancy finally gets a response of "hello" from Andrew, the next step might be to ask "How are you today?" and so on. These reciprocations can be extended musically as well through various songs and activities.

For example, the folk song "I Love My Little Rooster" (see figure 3.2) is often sung in early childhood and elementary music classrooms. Because the song asks students to name the sound of an animal and then add one animal to each verse, joint attention can be rehearsed in an inclusion setting. If Andrew were in this classroom, he might be asked to remember the rooster because it is the animal named most often. At first, the music educator and students will probably need to wait at the end of each verse for Andrew to make the rooster sound before they sing. By using this cadential point in the music, the impetus for participation is even further heightened. Each subsequent verse begins with a child (or the teacher) choosing an animal sound. The students sing that verse (e.g., ROAR (lion) and then add the rooster sound to end the verse. The song/game continues in an additive fashion until the students (or teacher!) are having difficulty remembering the order and sounds of the animals.

I Love My Little Rooster

American Folk Song

Figure 3.2
"I Love My Little Rooster." American folk song

These activities should be carefully planned with the goal of extending the conversation (either verbally or musically) ultimately expanding joint attention and social interaction between the music teacher, the student, and his peers. However, music teachers should not force the issue or be in a hurry to extend these interactions. Remember that a musical goal can be divided into infinitely discrete steps for a student with autism. It is a delicate dance between expecting and teaching appropriate response and social interaction, vs. making a child feel inadequate for not responding. Music teachers should use caution and common sense when encouraging an increase in joint attention. In addition, they should consult with the special education team about the level of expectations for these types of responses. More information regarding this concept is discussed later.

CAUTIONARY CONSIDERATIONS

- Nonverbal forms of communication can be valuable ways to communicate with a student who has autism. Many young children with autism are taught to use American Sign Language and other forms of communication.
- Ask for and expect eye contact from students with autism. This will help them understand appropriate communication skills.
- A student may not cease using echolalia during instruction. It may take a while for him or her to engage in the lesson and feel comfortable in the learning environment. Consult with special educators as to what would be an appropriate way to curb echolalia in your classroom. This is assuming that it is disruptive to overall student learning.

RECEPTIVE AND EXPRESSIVE LANGUAGE SKILLS

Receptive language (the ability to receive and process verbal information) and expressive language (the ability to express and articulate understanding) are intertwined skills that must be evident as children learn to communicate. Almost everyone has a stronger set of receptive language skills compared with their expressive language skills. Unfortunately, for many children on the autism spectrum, one or both of these skill sets are greatly delayed. This has a profound affect on the communication development of children with autism, which in turn, affects learning.

Receptive Language

Receptive and expressive language relies on early prelanguage skills learned by young children. Typically, students who do not understand language rely on facial expressions, tone of voice, and symbolic syntax to discern meaning. For a student diagnosed with autism, these secondary channels are sometimes unclear or absent. If the student is unable to use those channels to discern meaning, she is significantly limited in her ability to comprehend language in a receptive manner. This also may be one of many reasons for lack of eye contact in a student on the spectrum. The inability to use these clues is also part of the ToM mentioned earlier. Students with autism struggle with commonly used gestures, tone of voice, and facial expressions to convey meaning (Siegel, 2003).

Students with autism are able to use nonverbal communication to demonstrate pleasure or displeasure with events and activities. However, possessing this communicative ability does not mean that they will be able to read the same or similar expressions when used by others—the natural, nonverbal expressions we all make in response to events in our lives. These nonverbal gestures and expressions are prerequisites to the ability to speak, and it is essential for us to understand them as we teach students with autism in music classrooms.

Students with autism also do not always perceive sound the way other children do. They sometimes hear words and music as noise rather than language. The experience can include a complete disconnect between sound as communication and sound as noise (or disruption of thoughts). Some students are unable to hear differences in melodic lines and instead hear these sounds as white noise. Students are then also unable to discern whether an aural sound is meaningful or not, thus interrupting their ability to receive the appropriate information. These sensory differences are not easy to diagnose in some students with autism, but are still an opportunity for astute music educators to observe the reactions (or absence of reactions) of a student to various aural input.

For example, Vinnie, who has high-functioning autism, was diagnosed by a specialist in aural discernment as being unable to hear music as sets of tones when he was in third grade. His general music teacher was a highly skilled music educator who was Kodály-certified. In class, Vinnie was enthusiastic, yet often unsuccessful, in singing and in decoding melodies. His music teacher was perplexed because Vinnie was intelligent, interested, and definitely participated during music. She thought that attention, perhaps, was the cause of his inability to match pitch and to respond correctly to questions during instruction. Once the sensory expert began to use strategies to define and ameliorate his aural dyspraxia (when tones and music do not sound like music), Vinnie began to understand the music for the very first time! By the time Vinnie was in fifth grade, he was a leader in the school choir, and other students often relied on him for pitches when singing in parts.

The "noise" experienced by students with autism who are unable to differentiate sound can overwhelm them, and teachers may observe these students with their hands over their ears in a distressed state. When students with autism experience "word noise", they quickly become unable to process any information and may then engage in tantrums. This sensory overstimulation is commonly misunderstood as a behavior issue. Conversely, it is a demonstration of the needs of the student as a result of sensory overload in a classroom. Teachers should not assume a child is ignoring a request or direction or that noncompliance is the issue (National Research Council, 2001). An inability to recognize language signals (sound or sight) is a powerful inhibitor to the ability to understand and/or follow directions.

When a young child indicates a want or need by pointing, it is often a very valid early indicator of expressive language. This necessary early gesture is most often absent in young children with autism. To be able to point, a young child must know which item he desires, understand that your eyes will follow his eyes, and that you will be able to see the item he is pointing toward as he expresses his request. These ToM activities can be extremely difficult to teach to young children with autism and will probably not be acquired without many rehearsals over a long period of time. Children who are unable to make these connections are demonstrating "mindblindness." While young children learn a great deal about the world around them from the reactions of those around them to gestures like pointing, a child with autism will not be able to engage in these informal learning experiences because he does not understand how to express his interest in or need for a specific item. The thousands of short learning lessons that neurotypical children experience do not occur naturally for a child with autism (National Research Council, 2001).

Expressive Language Development (Cause and Effect)

One early form of expressive language demonstrated by all young children is the temper tantrum. A temper tantrum is a universal (and age negated) sign that the person presenting the tantrum is frustrated and possibly angry. When a young child has autism and is unable to express his wants and needs using nonverbal or verbal communication, frustration can mount into a torrent of screams and tears. Students with autism want to communicate and are often extremely frustrated that they are unable to do so. These types of behaviors will be mentioned throughout this text. However, having a communication plan will assist with decreasing the frequency of meltdowns and tantrums.

Most children begin to develop expressive language skills immediately. After crying to express discomfort, a child's ability to babble is an initial developmental milestone in expressive language. All infants babble at some point, and physicians and speech therapists look for this behavior as an indicator of emerging language skills. In addition, when a neuro-typical child says "mama," a powerfully reinforcing effect often results. The person who hears it often responds with attention, praise, smiles, and more language. This child quickly learns that language is a way to motivate those around him. Thus, more language is developed (i.e., "Dada") to further engage others. The cause and effect (action and consequence) cycle continues as language develops (Siegel, 2003). However, if the child never offers these utterances through babble, he or she will never receive such reinforcement. This is one reason many children with autism have speech delays. This pattern can be considered similar to the eye gaze and joint attention issues discussed earlier in this chapter. If a child does not receive feedback for behaviors, he does not learn the power and importance of those behaviors, nor does he rehearse them as other children do early in their lives. Therefore, the speech delays compound daily along with the joint attention and eye gaze delays, as children with autism fall further behind in their early childhood development.

When it is suspected that a child may have autism, the testing process generally includes standardized tests of language ability (e.g., Preschool Language Scales, Peabody Picture Vocabulary Test). These tests are often very accurate when determining levels of receptive and expressive language in neurotypical children. They can be unreliable, however, when used with children who have autism. Inherent in autism is an inability or a deficit in ability to perceive and express information. It can be very difficult to accurately assess a child who cannot sit and attend during an assessment. Parents are sometimes asked to assist in this process, as there are reliable measures that can be completed by parents to assess the language acquisition level of their child (Siegel, 2003). The lesson to learn, however, is to take each standardized test result with slight skepticism. Because each child with autism is different, a standardized test is perhaps not the best single option to utilize to measure levels of functioning and aptitude for the future.

STRATEGIES FOR MUSIC EDUCATORS IN EXPRESSIVE AND RECEPTIVE LANGUAGE

To assist students within the music classroom, music teachers should attempt to extend the conversation (including musical conversations) for as long as possible. For example, during a hello song, instead of just singing a student's name, add "what did you have for lunch?" and then, later, "who did you sit by?" When these activities are repeated over time, these extensions often become longer, with increased reciprocity.

Music teachers may also examine their delivery of musical material. Self-reflection is important. Music teachers may themselves ask questions that include: How many words am I using? How fast is my pace? Am I making eye contact with my students? Does Johnny understand that I am happy with his progress? Does Adam understand when I am looking at him to be quiet? Am I breaking down my instructions into a logical sequence? All these areas are important in strengthening a music teacher's ability to communicate with a student with autism.

STEPS TO EFFECTIVE COMMUNICATION WITH STUDENTS WITH AUTISM IN THE MUSIC CLASSROOM

Figure 3.3 was developed to illustrate steps used to encourage development of communication within the music classroom. Considering these four steps when planning accommodations will improve overall communication between music teachers and students with autism.

Step 1: Establish Eye Contact

Step 1 is to encourage eye contact as much as possible. Insist on this as a part of your greetings, reciprocations, and joint attention. Try to extend

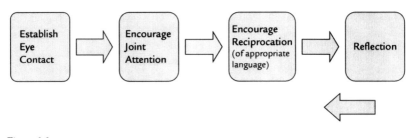

Figure 3.3
Steps to Affective Communication in the Music Classroom
Source: Hammel & Hourigan (2011)

these interactions as much as possible. However, be cautious regarding the current limitations a student with autism may have. Begin with small steps and work to lengthen each day as the student is able to respond.

Step 2: Encourage Joint Attention

Step 2 is to further encourage joint attention. Attempt to maintain student attention and extend this attention during the lesson for as long as possible. If you obtain an appropriate response to a question or a musical example, ask a second question, or ask the student to provide another response. In addition, use items of interest to help extend attention. For example, if the student likes to play a hand drum, use this instrument in the lesson. Use the patterns he plays as a basis for continuing the rhythm lesson. Remember to collect data as you teach to demonstrate progress and provide information for future interactions

Step 3: Encourage Reciprocation

Step 3 is to encourage reciprocation. Keep track of the number of times the student has taken turns within a conversation (data collection). Again, attempt to extend this as long as possible. For example, add elements to the conversation that may spark his interest inside or outside the lesson. Also, be in touch with the special education staff for ideas they use in other areas. The back and forth dialogue that comes with normal conversation will improve. It may appear to be scripted or learned behavior at first (i.e., she simply repeats the response she has learned each time). However, after a while, the student may learn to add her own fragments and components to the conversation (musical or nonmusical). This practice of learned responses, and eventual transfer to improvised responses, is a vital sequence as the student becomes successful using verbal communication.

Finally, reflecting on events that took place during the lesson is some-thing students with autism struggle with as well, yet it is especially impor-tant for retention of musical material. Students have been successful when asked to write, draw, or say a sentence or two about what they have learned. For students who struggle with communication, use of laminated cards from which they can choose a response, or simple one- or two-word phrases given by a teacher are also effective. These strategies can be very valuable in the retention of information learned during class. Informal closure and assessment strategies reinforce retention of musical skills and understand-ings, and allow music teachers to design a formative assessment for future planning of accommodated lessons.

AUGMENTATIVE AND ALTERNATIVE COMMUNICATION FOR STUDENTS WITH AUTISM

Because communication is difficult for students with autism, there are many alternative communication devices on the market for use in the music classroom. Many of these devices are available and in use in school districts. The districts probably own or can obtain most of the needed com-munication devices through special education cooperative programs. The Picture Exchange Communication System (PECS) is one tool that works well within the music classroom. PECS is a system of picture icons to use in place of or along with verbal prompts (see figure 3.4).

Figure 3.4
Picture Exchange Communication System Icons provided by Boardmaker
Source: The Picture Communications Symbols ©1981–2011 by Mayer-Johnson LLC. All Rights Reserved Worldwide. Used with permission. Boardmaker® is a trademark of Mayer-Johnston LLC.

Many special education programs own Boardmaker, a software program that creates PECS icons. There are many musical examples available for music educators. PECS allows students who have expressive language challenges an opportunity to communicate. Instead of verbally expressing their intent, they can point to the picture icon to express themselves (as illustrated in the example earlier in the chapter). This has been a successful tool for students with autism for many years and can be used by students to ask for assistance, request a break, or convey a need, or by teachers for assessment purposes.

A new resource available in the area of assistive technology is called a Skoog (see figure 3.5; available for purchase at www.skoogmusic.com). This cube-shaped device is revolutionary in its ability to create a variety of sounds that include articulation, bowing styles, and multiple notes at one time. In addition, it can be used with any MIDI or sound file. The soft outer shell is designed to produce sound when touched by any part of a student's body. For students with great physical challenges, this instrument can be their opportunity to participate in instrumental settings. It connects to a computer via a USB cable and provides musical independence for students who may otherwise have great difficulty participating in an ensemble or other group music setting.

In addition, the invention of apps for the iPad and iPhone have drastically changed the ability of students with autism to communicate. There are apps for PECS icons, picture schedules, and other communicative devices. A suggested list is available at http://tinyurl.com/7xseuf2, provided

Figure 3.5
A Skoog
Source: Courtesy of Skoog Music, www.skoogmusic.com.

by iTaalk, as well as at a new website assembled for the Children with Exceptionalities Special Research Interest Group (SRIG) for the National Association for Music Education (NAfME) at https://sites.google.com/site/exceptionalitiessrig.

Sign language is also often used with children with language challenges. It is taught in tandem with verbal cues to reinforce language skills. Some music educators teach children with autism who can sign but cannot yet express language verbally.

COMMUNICATION INTERRUPTIONS (A FAILURE TO COMMUNICATE)

There may be times when a communication interruption occurs with a student on the spectrum. This can lead to a meltdown and cause disruptive behavior. As mentioned previously, these incidents can also result in safety issues for the music teacher, other students, and the student with autism.

Vignette 3.2
AN EXAMPLE OF A COMMUNICATION INTERRUPTION

Jacob entered music class with a paraprofessional and the rest of his class. Everyone sat down in a circle and began to sing the hello song. Out of the corner of his eye, Jacob spotted his favorite conga drum. The class had just completed a drumming unit (which Jacob absolutely loved).

Jacob proceeded to stand up, walk to the drum, and begin to play. He didn't ask permission and Mrs. Smith (the music teacher) was not planning to use drums that particular day. In fact, she is known to take pride in showing her students the best way to care for and respect these instruments.

When Jacob reached the drum and started to play very loudly, Mrs. Smith walked to lead Jacob back to the rest of his class. Jacob then said, "Play drum?". Mrs. Smith tried to explain that when they finished the lesson, Jacob could play the drum. However, Jacob did not comprehend the idea of "first music lesson—then play drum."

Jacob thought Mrs. Smith did not understand that he was requesting to play the drum. Mrs. Smith, on the other hand, understood exactly what he wanted. Jacob did not understand, however, that Mrs. Smith was saying not now, later. The exchange spiraled out of control and his paraprofessional had to remove him from the room.

CAUTIONARY CONSIDERATIONS

- Noncompliance may actually be sensory overload, anxiety, or a communication difference. Look deep into the intent of the episode. Also, retrace your lesson plan or schedule of events for that day.
- Do not overlook the interests of the student when planning for teaching. Often, this helps them stay engaged in the lesson. Also, the sequence of your lesson (as well as the students schedule) is often important. Do not introduce a new event or schedule change without preparing the student with autism for the change.
- There are many ways to use technology to assist when communicating with students with autism. Some are mentioned in this chapter. However, there are many others. Speak to your special education staff about such needs.

Communication gaps are often the cause of these events. In these instances, consider the situation through the eyes of the student. There are times when teachers do not consider impulse control, obsessive behavior, and language obstacles when evaluating a situation in the classroom. Vignette 3.2 is an example of this. Often, a music teacher uses phrases that are too long or directions that are unclear.

In Mrs. Smith's case, a simple reinforcement of first/then as a concept will be needed. Hopefully, Mrs. Smith consulted the special education team to find behavioral reinforcers, picture icons, and techniques that can be built into the schedule to use with Jacob.

Even with use of the foregoing strategies, it is possible that this kind of event will happen again. However, if Mrs. Smith were to provide a clear schedule of music events (in word or picture format) and reinforce them in the manner most effective for Jacob, the occurrence of these kinds of breakdowns in communication would be less frequent (and may disappear). When students are aware of first/then or how long they are asked to comply with the requests of a teacher before they are provided their reinforcer (activity or item), they are more likely to remain engaged in classroom activities.

SOCIAL STORIES

Social stories are another alternative for assisting students with autism in the area of communication. Social stories were discussed in a vignette about Melany in chapter 2. Social stories are short stories written for a person with autism to help them understand and behave appropriately in specific social situations (Gray, 2004). Students with autism can experience immense anxiety in regard to understanding their schedule. Therefore, social stories can help music teachers communicate about a special event or change in activities. Social stories are written, not necessarily to change behavior, but to alleviate anxiety involved in understanding social situations (Gray, 2004). If a new event occurs (e.g., music class, a performance, a trip), providing a social story about it in advance can make a tremendous difference. The story will be effective if it is created in enough time for a student to comprehend and rehearse prior to the situation or event. Teachers often start telling the social story repeatedly in advance of the event and ask the student questions about what is going to happen (based on the student's level of comprehension).

Figure 3.6 is an example of a social story to be used for an upcoming concert. Hopefully, the social story shown in figure 3.6 will assist Spencer with being able to predict what will happen at a concert. Communicating what will happen at this event allows Spencer to feel some control over the situation. Obviously, surprises happen; however, social stories provide a sense of normalcy and understanding for students like Spencer. Social stories can also be accompanied by pictures of the event. These authentic photos can also assist with the transition the student is being asked to make.

+ Spencer will arrive at school (provide a picture of the school or show Spencer walking into school).
+ Spencer will walk down the hall to Mrs. Smith's rehearsal room.
+ Spencer will hang his coat on the coat rack (again, show picture of the his coat hook).
+ Spencer will see Mrs. Smith (with picture of Mrs. Smith).
+ Spencer will go get his music folder and join the group in the rehearsal room.
+ Mrs. Smith will warm up the choir (picture of the choir singing).
+ Spencer will go with his choir on the stage (picture of stage).
+ There will be lots of people and warm lights.
+ Mrs. Smith will be by your side if you need help.
+ The choir will sing Elijah Rock.
+ The people will clap loudly.
+ It is okay if you cover your ears.
+ The choir will sing Simple Gifts.
+ The people will clap loudly.
+ It is okay if you cover your ears again.
+ Spencer, Mrs. Smith, and the choir will leave the stage.
+ Spencer will be allowed to sit with his parents.

Figure 3.6
A Social Story

Social stories can also be musical. The following is an example of a social story that appears in *Music and Special Education* (Adamek & Darrow, 2010, 199) set to the "ABC Song":

> *Wait your turn, wait today,*
> *Then you'll have a chance to play.*
> *First it's her, then it's him*
> *Round the circle back to you.*
> *Wait your turn, wait today,*
> *Then you'll have a chance to play*

CONCLUSION

Communication is a pivotal window that must be opened to enable students with autism to participate in music. It is imperative that music teachers establish a communication system with students. These strategies are often very effective when they coincide with communication systems already established in other classes. Music teachers are strongly encouraged consult with the special education team, classroom teachers, and parents to establish a comfortable learning environment for students with autism in the music classroom.

REFERENCES

Adamek, M. S., & Darrow, A. A. (2010). *Music in special education* (2nd ed.). Silver Spring, MD: American Music Therapy Association.

Baron-Cohen, S. (2000). Theory of mind and autism. In S. Baron-Cohen, H. Tager-Flusberg, & D. Cohen (eds.), *Understanding other minds: Perspectives from developmental cognitive neuroscience* (2nd ed., pp. 3–20). Oxford, England: Oxford University Press.

Gray, C. (2004). Social stories 10.0: The new defining criteria and guidelines. *Jennison Autism Journal,* 15(4), 2–21.

Heflin, J. L., & Alaimo, D. F. (2007). *Students with autism spectrum disorders.* Upper Saddle River, NJ: Pearson Education.

National Research Council (NRE) (2001). *Educating children with autism.* Division of Behavioral and Social Sciences and Education. Washington, DC: National Academy Press.

Siegel, B. (2003). *Helping children with autism learn.* New York: Oxford University Press.

Sigman, M., & Ruskin, E. (1999). Continuity and change in the social competence of children with autism, down syndrome, and developmental delays. *Monographs of the Society in Research in Child Development,* 64, 1–114.

Tiegerman, E., & Primavera, L. (1984). Imitating the autistic child: Facilitating communicative gaze disorder. *Journal of Autism and Developmental Disorders,* 14, 27–38.

Volkmar, F. R. & Klin, A, (2005). Issues in the classification of autism and related conditions. In F. Volkmar, R. Paul, A. Klin, & D. Cohen (eds.), *Handbook of autism and pervasive developmental disorders* (pp. 5–41). Hoboken, NJ: John Wiley & Sons.

DISCUSSION QUESTIONS

1. Reexamine vignette 3.1. Now that you have read this chapter, what strategies would you use with Andrew in Mr. Clancy's music classroom?
2. Examine vignette 3.2. Based on what you have learned from this chapter, how would you defuse this communication interruption?
3. What kind of communication alternatives would be useful in your music classroom (or future music classroom)?
4. What musical strategies can be used to extend a conversation?
5. What musical strategies can be used to encourage joint attention?
6. What musical strategies can be used to encourage reciprocation?

CHAPTER 4

Understanding Cognition and Students with Autism Spectrum Disorder

---

CHAPTER OVERVIEW

One of the most unique attributes of students with autism is the distinctive manner by which they think. This chapter sheds light into the cognitive world of students with autism in the music classroom. The following topics are included:

- Theory of mind
- Central coherence
- Executive function
- Joint attention (and cognition)
- Music cognition and students with autism

One of the highlights of teaching music to children with autism is the opportunity to discover the distinctive way they think. Some students may be able to tell you every finite musical detail about a piece of music or remember everything they have ever learned about a composer. Another student may have unique musical abilities that are above and beyond those of the typical music student. This is due to the unique way a person with autism develops in the area of cognition.

Modern science has linked autism to the interplay among genes, the brain, and the environment (Hill & Frith, 2003). The brain of a person with autism is known to have structural abnormalities (Bauman & Kemper, 1994). Specifically, research has shown that persons with autism have reduced "neuronal cell size and increased cell-packing density in the limbic

---

Vignette 4.1
CINDY

Cindy is an eighth grader in Mrs. Henderson's choir. Mrs. Henderson has noticed that Cindy can tell her every minute detail about the composer and composition they are singing. For example, when they performed the Brahms "The May Night." Cindy could tell her when Brahms was born, the town he was from, the other composers he worked with, and many of his other works. However, when asked what "The May Night" was about, Cindy returned to telling Mrs. Hendricks about all of the facts about Brahms.
  Discussion:
  1. Why can't Cindy tell Mrs. Henderson about "The May Night"?
  2. What can Mrs. Hendricks do to help Cindy comprehend the more abstract concepts of the music?

---

system critical to emotional and social behavior" (p. 282). This may be the reason for the different ways people with autism function cognitively.

Another way of looking at the difference between a typical functioning brain and the brain of a person with autism is the way genes in the brain express themselves. Specifically, within the cerebral cortex and the frontal lobe, where it is known that the brain processes judgment, creativity, emotions and speech, and in the temporal lobe, which also regulates hearing, language, and the processing and interpretation of sound. It is thought that in a typical brain, genes are responsible for developing tissue that assists the brain in these processes.

The research on the autistic brain is still in its infancy. However, in a recent study by Dr. Daniel Geshwind, a leading researcher of autism at the University of California, Los Angeles, a team of researchers discovered consistent differences in how genes in autistic and in healthy brains encode information. But the research team also found that gene-expression patterns were similar in most, though not all, brains of people with autism. In a typical brain, genes in specific regions of the brain behave in different ways. In a person with autism, the same genes behave the same, regardless of where in the brain they are located.

In an interview with Canadian Television (CTV), Geschwind stated: "So you wouldn't necessarily expect that, and yet that's what we saw," Geschwind said a comparison of frontal and temporal lobes in healthy brains showed a 500-plus difference in genes expressed between the two brain regions. But in the autistic brains, "we only saw eight." In other words, between two different regions in a healthy brain, there are many different gene expressions that interpret the DNA of a person. In a brain of a person with autism, there is very little interpretation or expression of DNA in the brain across regions.

"In a healthy brain, hundreds of genes behave differently from region to region, and the frontal and temporal lobes are easy to tell apart," Geschwind noted. "We didn't see this in the autistic brain. Instead, the frontal lobe closely resembles the temporal lobe. Most of the features that normally distinguish the two regions had disappeared." Geschwind said many of the genes involved are neurodevelopmental genes, which are expressed during fetal growth midway through gestation. "So that's telling us that there is certainly a developmental component to (autism), a very early developmental component. That aspect of it looks like it would certainly be going on in utero" (May 2011 interview, CTV: http://www.ctv.ca/CTVNews/ Health/20110526/autism-brain-genes-110525/).

When it comes to cognitive function and people with autism, much of the research points to genetic and neurodevelopmental challenges that occur early in life. These challenges affect a person's ability to process judgment, creativity, emotions, speech, and language, as well as the processing and interpretation of sensory information. Consequently, these difficulties have a profound affect on the ability of a child to learn.

What does this mean for music teachers? Students with autism in the music classroom receive, process, and express neuroinformation differently than their typical peers, especially in the areas just mentioned. The good news is that the literature shows how and why these processes occur and how students can be accommodated. Based on this research, this chapter examines the basic functions and abnormalities of the brain and students with autism and how these idiosyncrasies can be accommodated in the music classroom.

CAUTIONARY CONSIDERATIONS

- Do not assume a student with cognitive challenges also has challenges in the area of communication. There are many children who have strong communication skills but are challenged in the area of cognition (and vice versa). Remember, each child usually has unique cognitive and communication skills.

THEORY OF MIND AND COGNITION

As we mentioned in chapter 3, people often communicate with each other nonverbally, through glances, looks, raised eyebrows, or body language. Cognitively, these indicators can be used to understand or predict the intent of another person. This is where ToM is a bridge between communication and cognition and is the foundation for social intelligence (Peterson, Wellman, & Liu, 2005).

Typical-developing people can predict another person's actions or intent by assuming their beliefs or state of mind. A child can infer certain beliefs and emotions from just reading a face or body language, or by assuming a logical sequence of events. For example, a student named Michael anxiously raises his hand in music class because he knows the answer to a question. All the other students in classroom can see that Michael probably knows the answer, is feeling anxious about answering the question, and is trying the get the attention of the music teacher.

On the other hand, asking Susie (who has been diagnosed with autism) a simple question such as "what does Michael want?" may result in Susie explaining what *she* wants instead. If you ask her "how is Michael feeling?" she may explain how she is feeling, and so on. Susie may have trouble

---

Vignette 4.2
JOY

Joy is in first grade at Falls Elementary School. The teacher is singing "The north wind doth blow and we shall have snow, and what will poor Robin do then? He'll sit in the barn to keep himself warm and hide his head under his wing. Poor thing." "How does Robin feel?", the teacher asks. Joy is unable to understand why Robin would be sad when it snows or is cold. The teacher wants the students to choose a tempo and style of singing. Joy thinks about how happy she is when it snows. Sometimes she gets to stay home because there is no school. She loves to play in the snow. Also, when it is cold, she gets to wear her pretty blue coat that is soft. When she wears her pretty coat, she doesn't get scratched by people touching her skin. The coat is one of her favorite things about cold weather. Joy continues to misunderstand and begins to pull the hair of the girl in front of her because she is no longer interested in the lesson. She is then removed from the classroom by her paraprofessional.

Discussion:
- What can the teacher do to help Joy understand the feelings of others (e.g., the Robin)?
- How can the teacher expand Joy's engagement in the lesson?

supposing what Michael may want or how he feels. Understanding Michael's desires or needs is very abstract and is a struggle for many students with autism.

In music we often work in the abstract. We may interpret lyrics or emotions. We might examine why a unique population would compose or use music to express their wants or needs. These are very abstract concepts for a person with autism, and because of the skills they require, students with autism are often unable to engage in this type of cognitive process. This was described in the vignette 4.2 about Joy. Some further classroom examples include the concept of spirituals, nationalistic music, music for specific situations (ballet music, leitmotifs, funeral or wedding music), and poems set to music. Students with autism often require specific transfers of information using a formula to assist them. They also must have repeated practice to assimilate new information and ways of thinking. Social stories work well here as students can rehearse approaching an understanding until they are able to make that transfer without the use of a social story. Here is an example:

Jonah is in fifth-grade music. His class is learning about the use of leitmotifs in music. Jonah has a very difficult time attaching characters to music and becomes frustrated. His music teacher chooses Charlie Brown as a topic for Jonah because he loves watching the Charlie Brown movies and looking at the cartoons. She creates a social story book to assist Jonah as he begins to rehearse the classroom behaviors the students will engage in during this unit. The social story shows pictures of the Charlie Brown characters and Jonah looking at them while listening to the music. Jonah is able to repeat the book every day and as often as he likes to be able to participate appropriately with his classmates in music class. In the book Jonah uses, the pictures show that Jonah is not frustrated, anxious, or tense when learning. The last page of the book shows Jonah smiling because he has listened to the music and studied the pictures.

Leitmotifs in the music of Charlie Brown: Each motif can be recorded and made into an MP3 file. The student can listen to the short motif while looking at the picture of the character. Pictures or short statements about the specific Charlie Brown character can be read as the child becomes familiar with the specific musical idea. Slowly, additional characters from the series can be added, with their specific musical motives. After repeated practice, the student can begin to identify the musical ideas and attach them to the character. This simple process can then be used to introduce more complex musical ideas and concepts.

Figure 4.1
Lesson Plan Example: Leitmotifs (Charlie Brown)

WEAK CENTRAL COHERENCE

Another aspect of autism that affects many children is described as "weak central coherence." Hill and Frith (2003) defined this concept as "a tendency to focus on the local rather than the global aspects of an object of interest" (p. 284). It is also called "central coherence theory." It is thought to come from an inability to organize incoming information. For example, a typical student can listen to a story and be able to give you a basic summary of it including the main characters, plot line, and setting. People who have a weak central coherence will be able to give you many small details about a story but are not able to connect them to give you the overall meaning. This is very common among people with autism.

The cause of a weak central coherence is not yet fully determined, although many researchers feel it is caused by weak or different connections in the brain. Researchers use central coherence to explain why persons with autism may have enhanced skills in art, music, calculation, and memory (Happe, 2005, 640). In fact, one out of every ten persons with autism has these enhanced skills. This may be a result of many different neural pathways that develop in the brain of a person with autism.

A good example of how weak central coherence might manifest itself in music is in the text of a choral work. A child may be able to hear the piece once and sing it back to you perfectly in tune and with great diction. She may be able to remember everything that you told her to do in rehearsal. However, in a performance of the work she cannot focus on the balance or intonation of the group and may have difficulty interpreting the overall meaning of the piece of music. She may also have difficulty understanding the nuances necessary to provide an expressive performance based on the emotional moment that occurs in certain sections of the work. This is an essential part of active participation in a large ensemble, yet this student may only focus on her own individual performance rather than function as part of the group.

STRATEGIES FOR ASSISTING WITH CENTRAL COHERENCE CHALLENGES

Many music educators may have taught a student who has attributes similar to those just mentioned. That studenet may have perfect pitch or be able to express music extraordinarily well in the most technical of situations. In the area of central coherence, the challenge for many students with autism is synthesizing the surface-level skills (e.g., notes, rhythms, terms) into a global, emotional experience that has meaning. Asking a student to talk about the meaning of the lyrics or the intent of the musical timbre is a true test of understanding a technique or compositional setting.

In these situations, as in the Charlie Brown example, start with small elements and expectations. Begin by asking specific reflective questions about the music. Why is this section loud? The student may need to rehearse this question multiple times using a social story book or set of musical examples that demonstrate the difference between loud and soft. Once the loud and soft concepts are familiar to the student, the next step is to begin teaching the gradations of dynamic contrast in the same manner. In the beginning, a similar timbre for the examples will be clearer to the student. Once the student understands the concept of dynamic contrast, adding a variety of timbres will begin to make this skill transferrable to other musical situations. By using various timbres, the student will then learn that dynamic contrast exists in different settings.

While building this specific skill, students can also be lead through the ways emotion is conveyed in music. This involves an entirely separate set of skills for a student with autism, as each step is discrete and separate in his understanding. Allowing the student to describe how dynamics and timbre are used to convey a specific emotion lets the student rehearse (with help from the teacher) how someone feels when she hears or writes music that sounds a specific way. Questions like "what did the composer mean when she wrote these words?" can be added to the dynamic contrast and timbre discussions. Then, the conversation can be extended from there. This teaching sequence can be taught as other students are also learning about composer intent and use of timbre and dynamics.

The beauty of an active inclusion classroom is that student needs can be met in a differentiated structure while all the students are learning according to their needs. Continuing to increase the level of comprehension requires students to develop mental stamina. If students are not continually asked to think and process information, they may lose the ability to reflect on these global musical ideas. Repeated practice with specific questions and skills can dramatically improve the ability of a student with autism to consider more abstract questions and to respond reflectively during a music class or ensemble.

CAUTIONARY CONSIDERATIONS

- Remember that repetition is powerful, and students with autism often need more repetition than students who are neurotypical.
- Weak central coherence or central coherence theory is not associated with intelligence. Therefore, music teachers should not assume that if someone has weak central coherence, they are not intelligent.

EXECUTIVE FUNCTION

Executive function refers to the use of several functions in the brain such as "planning, working memory, impulse control, shifting set, and the initiation and monitoring of action as well as the inhibition of prepotent responses" (Hill & Frith, 2003, p. 285). These basic functions are thought to be connected to the prefrontal activity in the brain. Figure 4.2 explains these prefrontal functions for clarity.

In persons with autism, one or all of the basic, or *executive*, functions can be impaired or lost. Because of this, students may have difficulty with basic day-to-day class functions such as taking turns, remembering creative movement, understanding rules, and collaborative learning (Ozonoff, South, & Provencal, 2005).

As music teachers, it is important that we examine these functions and discuss strategies with other teachers who work with that student. A primary teaching skill is the ability to define precisely the executive function challenge a student is experiencing. Once this challenge is identified, a

---

Vignette 4.3
BERT

Bert plays saxophone in the Sundance High School Marching Band. He loves being a part of the band; however, he often has great difficulty with cognitive planning when he is asked to prepare for rehearsal. Some days, Bert must travel from his history classroom to the band practice field for class. He is, frankly, overwhelmed at the cognitive tasks required to successfully find his way. He is allowed to leave the class two minutes early to avoid the noise and motion that is common in high-school hallways. Once he arrives at the band room, the task becomes more daunting. The instrument room, even when carefully organized and labeled, looks like a maze to Bert. He has great difficulty finding his instrument, and his folder is sometimes accidentally put in a different slot. Once he finds his drill chart, he can become completely engrossed with counting the dots on each page. Bert does not even notice as the rest of the students enter the room, gather their materials, and head to the field. His immediate need to make sure each page has the same amount of dots can preempt his cognitive planning. The result is that section leaders often find him standing in the instrument room counting dots long after he was due to report to the field. The result of this experience causes Bert to become extremely agitated and he is, once again, redirected to his resource room for "think time" with his teacher.

Working Memory: The term *working memory* refers to a brain system that provides temporary storage and manipulation of the information necessary for such complex cognitive tasks as language comprehension, learning, and reasoning.

Planning: A scheme, program, or method prepared before the accomplishment of an objective.

Impulse Control: An inability to control actions. Impulse actions are typically preceded by feelings of tension, rage, and excitement and followed by a sense of relief and gratification that is also—but not always— accompanied by guilt or remorse.

Shifting Set: The process of updating or "shifting" cognitive strategies in response to changes in the environment.

Initiation and Monitoring of Action: Refers to the ability of a person to initiate and monitor their own actions.

Inhibition of Prepotent Response: This involves deliberately inhibiting dominant, automatic responses. *Persons with Autism can have difficulty inhibiting a dominant response for a correct response.*

Figure 4.2
Prefrontal Functions of the Brain (Related to Executive Dysfunction)

teacher may begin adapting lessons appropriately. For example, if a student has difficulty planning, creating a task analysis that lists each discrete step in the process can be crucial.

Many students with autism respond favorably to a set of steps necessary to achieve a task. A visual set of reminders can be very useful in assisting a student in becoming more independent. One example is to consider the cognitive frustrations a student with autism may have upon entering a busy middle-school band room. The seemingly effortless movements of other students as they prepare for rehearsal can be even more upsetting for a student who is trying to be part of the culture of the classroom.

A pictorial classroom readiness book can be used in these instances. This book is often effective when pictures of the student performing each step are used. Students with autism often have great difficulty cognitively processing facial expressions and emotions of others. Because of this, the use of the student himself as the character in the readiness book is valuable. An example of the steps is shown in figures 4.3 through 4.8.

Joshua is able to use his book repeatedly until he has the steps to this process memorized. Some students with autism who are aware of the steps and routine, however, still appreciate knowing they are performing the activities appropriately. They then sometimes use the book for comfort and to ease anxiety because it is a familiar and positive item in their daily routine.

Figure 4.3
It is time for band. I need my music and my mallets. My music and my mallets are in my locker.

Figure 4.4
When I find my music, I need to close my locker. Now it is time to go to the band room!!

Figure 4.5
The band room is called the "instrumental rehearsal" room. It is room 152 down the hall from English class. It might be loud when I walk in. However, Mrs. Hannula will be there to help me

Figure 4.6
When I get to the band room I need to: Look at the board to see what we are playing, uncover the marimba, take out my mallets, and follow directions. I need to raise my hand if I need to take a break

Figure 4.7
This is the whiteboard where the directions will be written. If I have any questions, I will raise my hand

Figure 4.8
When band is over I need to get my music and my mallets and wait at the door for Mrs. Hannula

JOINT ATTENTION (AS IT RELATES TO COGNITION)

As seen in vignette 4.4, music learning is a social experience. In examining the cognitive needs of a student with autism, music educators must also remember the importance of music students learning from their peers. For decades, educators have known that students often learn more from capable peers than adults. In fact, one of pioneers of modern psychology L. S. Vygotsky wrote: "Children are capable of doing much more in collective activity or under the guidance of adults" (1978, p. 88). In other words, through imitation, joint attention to interests, and modeling *from peers* students can often learn more than from adults or teachers.

Vignette 4.4

MS. ANDERSON

Susan Anderson has taught at Wichita Middle School for 15 years. She is a conscientious and dedicated choral teacher. Her choirs are known for their outstanding performances as well as their advanced musicianship skills. Even Susan, with her experience, skills, and work ethic, was stymied when a class of students with autism was included in her seventh-grade beginning choir. Many of the students were nonverbal, and the few who did speak used one or two words to express their needs. Susan had been an enthusiastic supporter of inclusion, yet had never considered how it might affect her music program to have six students with autism join her fifth-period class.

Once the year began and she was able to assess the strengths of the students and their paraprofessionals, Susan began composing percussion parts for many of the choral pieces her seventh-grade students were singing. She struggled to make the parts meaningful and to increase the amount of communication her seventh-grade students experienced with the students with autism. She paired students and assigned each pair percussion parts by piece. Each student played percussion with a student with autism for one piece on the winter concert. Progress was slow, however, Susan had chosen her literature carefully and was able to gauge her rehearsal time to allow relationships to develop. She was amazed to see her students and their partners communicating using eye blinks, finger motions, and swallowing to perform their parts together. She knew that joint attention activities like these were not only good for her students with autism, they were also opportunities for social growth among her seventh-grade students. Susan immediately asked whether there were other students in the building who would like to be included for music.

Discussion:
- What adaptations or accommodations provided by Susan could you use in your classroom?

The lack of joint attention by students with autism leaves them at a disadvantage in the area of cognition. They fail to be interested in the common learning that happens in a group activity or project. They struggle to pick up on imitation cues or the modeling that happens in their learning groups. Therefore, as music educators, examining social learning as an accommodation for students with autism must be part of the picture.

Music is a social, cognitive, and collaborative activity. Music therapists often use music as a catalyst to improve joint-attention skills. As music educators, we should attempt to extend joint attention to improve ensemble rhythm, musical affect, collaborative performance, and other musical skills that require students with autism to communicate nonverbally.

As an example, many secondary music educators teach literature by choosing concepts to focus on during instruction. All these concepts are nonverbal. The vast majority of musicianship skills require joint attention and collaboration. Each student in an ensemble is learning these musical elements. It is the students with autism who are often left out of these experiences and are, once again, left behind while their peers gain musical understanding they will not possess.

When engaging in concept teaching, the use of time on task and joint attention monitoring can begin to open the world of abstract and highly aesthetic musicianship for students with autism. A carefully sequenced set of expectations, accompanied by cognitive skills training, is often effective. To begin, a music educator will probably wish to sequence a skill from the most basic level to the level of understanding expected of other students in the ensemble.

One concept used in secondary ensembles is balance. Students learn the appropriate balance of their ensemble, what the teacher expects, and how to personally, and as a section, balance with the rest of the group. In a string orchestra, this can be a primary goal as a teacher leads her students to be able to balance their sections independently, and with knowledge of the melodic and harmonic responsibilities at any given moment in a piece of music. Figure 4.9 shows some of the questions that can get the student thinking about balance issues. To consider a sequence for balance, and to craft a tool useful to extend joint attention and understanding for a student with autism, is one of the delightful challenges in an inclusive orchestra classroom.

MUSICAL COGNITION, PERCEPTION, AND RESPONSE IN STUDENTS WITH AUTISM

Children on the autistic spectrum often possess remarkable capability for and responsiveness to music compared with most other areas of their behavior, as well as in comparison with their peers (Sobol, 2004). Typically, children on

o Is my violin sound louder or softer than my stand partner's sound?
o Is my violin sound matching the sounds of the other second violins?
o Is my violin sound appropriate for this part of the music?
o Do I have the melody or the harmony?
o What is my job in this part of the music?
o Does my sound balance with the first violin part?
o Does my sound balance with the viola part?
o Does my sound balance with the cello part?
o Does my sound balance with the bass part?

Figure 4.9
Balance

the autistic spectrum "respond more frequently and appropriately to music than to other auditory stimuli" (Thaut, 1999). Music can weave into the everyday vernacular of a student with autism. Many are able to communicate musically before they can communicate verbally. Some students with autism display musical skill sets that are advanced compared with children their own age and demonstrate the ability to communicate needs and emotions through music when they may otherwise be unable to make these feelings known.

The research regarding music and autism paints a picture that is essential for music teachers to understand. Many children with autism have very advanced nonaffective musical skills (e.g., perfect pitch, advanced rhythm skills, tonal memory). However, as noted earlier, research has shown that persons with autism struggle with the emotional aspects of music (Allen & Heaton, 2010). This is not necessarily a direct result of autism. Researchers have shown that emotional responses to music typically match the verbal or mental age of a student. In other words, the more delayed a student is verbally or cognitively, the less likely he is to match his peers in a demonstrated emotional response to music (Heaton, Allen, Williams, Cummins, & Happe, 2008).

When working with students who have autism, we can become "deficit focused." Much of this book is focused instead on ameliorating the deficits of students with autism. It is sometimes a refreshing change of paradigm to focus on the assets and strengths a student with autism can bring to the music classroom. These are very real assets and can be used to improve the overall classroom culture and learning opportunities for all students.

As an example, a student with autism who has perfect pitch and/or an advanced ability in the area of tonal memory can benefit the ability of an entire tenor section to find and maintain its tonal center. That student may then become a section leader or the "keeper of the pitch" for the tenors. With this arrangement in place to encourage and build on the innate

---

CAUTIONARY CONSIDERATIONS

- Do not overlook the power of visual information to accompany aural and kinesthetic input. The more you can combine one or more of these delivery styles, the better.
- We cannot stress the importance of social interactions between students with autism and their peers enough. Students with autism often, because of their challenges, miss these opportunities.
- The aesthetic effect music can have for students with autism can be very powerful, although they may consume their music experiences differently. Just because they react or experience music differently does not mean their experience is any less than that of other students.

aptitude of a student with autism, the area of musical understanding can be enhanced for the student with ASD. This same student may struggle cognitively to understand musical nuance and expression. It is possible to simultaneously enhance the student's strengths and to develop strategies to address his challenges in an authentic and student-centered manner.

CONCLUSION

What does this mean for music teachers? A lesson to learn from this chapter is that each student with autism has a unique mind with an individual set of neural pathways that develop differently. Students with autism tend to be challenged by the abstract and have difficulty with impulses and self-monitoring skills. When adapting lessons or rehearsals, music teachers will be most successful if they delineate specific, affect-related music constructs as small, understandable concepts. In addition, requiring collaboration and joint attention among students, and between students and the teacher will strengthen a student with autism's ability to play or sing in an ensemble setting. These skills require the music teacher to be able to adapt lessons to include reflective questioning, constructivist thinking, and flexibility in teaching the craft of music.

REFERENCES

Allen, R. & Heaton, P. (2010). Autism, music, and the therapeutic potential of music in alexithymia. *Music Perception: An Interdisciplinary Journal,* 27(4), 251–261.

Bauman, M. L., & Kemper, K. L. (1994). Neuroanatomical observations of the brain and autism. In M. L. Bauman & K.L. Kemper (eds.), *The neurobiology of autism* (pp. 119–145). Baltimore, MD: Johns Hopkins University Press.

Happe, F. (2005). The weak central coherence account of autism. In F. R. Volkmar, R. Paul, Klin, & D. Cohen (eds.), *Handbook of autism and pervasive developmental disorders* (pp. 640–649). Hokoken, NJ: John Wiley & Sons.

Heaton, P., Allen, R., Williams, K., Cummins, O., & Happe, F. (2008). So social and cognitive deficits curtail musical understanding? Evdience from autism and down syndrome. *British Journal of Developmental Psychology, 26,* 171–182.

Hill, E. L., & Frith, U. (2003). Understanding autism: Insights from mind and brain. *Philosophical Transactions: Biological Sciences,* 358(1430), 281–289.

Ozonoff, S., South, M., & Provencal, S. (2005). Executive functions. In F. R. Volkmar, R. Paul, A. Klin, & D. Cohen (eds.), *Handbook of autism and pervasive developmental disorders* (pp. 606–627). Hokoken, NJ: John Wiley & Sons.

Peterson, C. C., Wellman, H. M., & Liu, D. (2005). Steps in theory of mind development for children with deafness or autism. *Child Development,* 76(2), 502–517.

Sobol, E. S. (2004). Loud, louder, loudest: Teaching the dynamics of life. In *Spotlight on Making Music with Special Learners,* MENC (ed.) (pp. 68–71). Reston, VA: MENC.

Thaut, M. H. (1999). Music therapy with autistic children. In W. B. Davis, K Gfeller, & M. Thaut (eds.), *An introduction to music therapy* (pp. 166–167), Boston: McGraw-Hill.

Vygotsky, L. S. (1978). *Mind and Society.* Cambridge, MA: Harvard University Press.

DISCUSSION QUESTIONS

1. What adaptations can you make to your music lessons/rehearsals to address theory of mind, central coherence, or joint attention concerns?
2. How can you adapt behavior expectations for a student who has executive-function challenges?
3. How can you extend joint attention in your music classroom?

CHAPTER 5

Classroom Behavior and Students with Autism

CHAPTER OVERVIEW

Understanding behavior and the intent of a behavior is key to successfully teaching music to children with autism. This chapter includes the following topics:
- Child behavior development and autism
- Typical behavior interventions and strategies used by special educators
- Outbursts, meltdowns and other disruptions
- How routine and schedule interact with a student with autism and his behavior

---

Behavior is one major challenge that emerges when teaching music to students with autism. Music teachers may have a student who has autism who does not conform to the day's activities, is not engaged with the music teacher or her classmates, or, in some cases, may protest her participation in music altogether. This can be very difficult for any teacher, especially music teachers. Music classes and ensembles usually contain larger numbers of students, combined with equipment to manipulate, and limited time to accomplish goals. Often, music teachers are assigned a student with autism without the proper information and support (Hammel, 1999). This chapter is designed to assist music teachers with these concerns.

Before we suggest strategies for successful management of behavior in your music classroom, it is appropriate to consider the typical behavioral development of a child and how it may differ for those with autism. In addition, it is fitting to review different behavioral intervention methods used with students on the autism spectrum. Many special educators are trained

---

Vignette 5.1
MR. DEVANE

Mr. Devane is beginning his year with a brand-new group of seventh-grade band students. All students gather their equipment and enter the room. At the teacher inservice the day before, Mr. Devane received an IEP about Mark. He learned that Mark has autism through talking with special education members, since his family freely shares the diagnosis. Mr. Devane begins the rehearsal with a concert F scale. As soon as he begins, Mark yells at Mr. Devane to "stop!" Mr. Devane is confused. He begins again. Mark yells "stop!" and puts his hands over his ears. Eventually Mark's paraprofessional takes Mark out of the room.

Mr. Devane is confused because Mark was in band last year. In fact, Mr. Devane attended the spring concert. He did not remember Mark having any outbursts or behavior issues.

Discussion:
1. What could Mr. Devane have done to prepare the rehearsal for Mark?
2. What should Mr. Devane do now that this behavior has occurred?

---

and use one or more of these methods. By understanding behavioral interventions and strategies used by colleagues in special education, the music teacher can apply behavior-management plans in the music classroom that are consistent across campus and familiar to the students.

It is vital for music educators to understand how communication, routine, and social skills are linked to behavior for students with autism. With an understanding of plans currently implemented in general and special education classrooms, and with support of the special education team, music teachers can develop their own behavior plans to foster the best learning environment for all students in the music classroom. We recommend that readers also examine chapter 5, "Developing a Student-Centered and Inclusive Classroom," in our book *Teaching Music to Students with Special Needs: A Label-Free Approach*. This chapter builds upon the basic tenets described there.

CHILD BEHAVIOR DEVELOPMENT AND STUDENTS WITH AUTISM

Many students with autism enter classrooms displaying delays in social and behavioral development. They may still be working through behavioral milestones that neurotypcial students usually accomplish before entering school at the prekindergarten or kindergarten level. Hodgdon (2003) explains: "It is typical for behavior challenges to occur during these years (prior to entering school) while children are developing personal discipline, self control, and decision making skills" (p. 8). Students with autism who attend music classes and are members of ensembles may still be working through such challenges as sleep routines, eating, toilet training, social skills, basic decision-making skills, self-control, and a fundamental sense of autonomy. When you are working with individual students with autism, we recommend examining the IEP and talking with the special education staff to learn other behavior goals being considered for that student as part of his overall academic and social goals.

If the diagnosis of autism has been delayed, and many behaviors that are completely appropriate for a student with autism have been mislabeled "bad" by teachers or parents, this will have affected the overall self-esteem and sense of worth of the child. The later the diagnosis for a child, the more damage can have occurred to the child's sense of self. It is important for music teachers to be sensitive to self-esteem issues.

Some music educators are not accustomed to considering these items when preparing lesson plans. However, if a student cannot master some of these challenges (e.g., personal discipline, self-control, decision-making skills), he will not be able to participate and learn music in a classroom or rehearsal setting without assistance. His inability to interact with teachers and peers will also be detrimental to the learning experience of other students. Therefore, teachers may need to accommodate for these not-yet-developed skills to foster an environment that creates music-learning opportunities for all students. For example, in the area of social behavior, music educators sometimes find success in teaching the social skill or goal as a game that students play. Once students are able to play the taking-turns game, or the choosing-a-partner game, or the finding-your-seat game, they are then ready to participate in activities that involve taking turns, choosing a partner, and being in a designated place within the classroom.

Younger students in an elementary general music class will need to learn the rules and procedures, such as taking turns during a game or activity. This definitely requires a certain level of self-control and can quite possibly be a skill every student in the class is learning to master. A student with autism may not have developed the self-control necessary to wait for a turn (e.g., to choose her rhythm sticks). A music teacher may need to gauge how long a student will be able to wait based on previous experience and the behaviors the child is exhibiting at that moment. Maybe Joseph chooses to go second instead of fifteenth. As Joseph begins to understand that everyone will get a turn to choose rhythm sticks, the teacher may allow him to wait longer before choosing his instrument to help him continue to develop self-control. These adaptations may be required in a music classroom based on typical child-behavior development. A difference can be that Joseph is in the fifth grade and is still learning this valuable behavior.

UNDERSTANDING APPLIED BEHAVIOR ANALYSIS AND DISCRETE TRIAL TRAINING

Many special educators, through undergraduate or graduate programs, are trained to use the principles of ABA when working with students on the autism spectrum, as well as with other students with special needs. ABA is "the process of applying sometimes tentative principles of behavior to the improvement of specific behaviors, and simultaneously evaluating whether or not any changes noted are indeed attributable to the process of application" (Baer, Wolf, & Risely, 1968). In other words, teachers and service providers who are steeped in this approach attempt to promote appropriate behavior through positive reinforcement.

In working with students on the spectrum, teachers and therapists work to master specific skill sets (including behaviors) through DTT. This pedagogy requires dividing skills (including behaviors) into very small parts and reinforcing positive behaviors. An example is teaching students to sort notes by note value. Students are asked to sort the note values, and when they are correct, they earn a reward. Teachers collect data on attempts and success rates (Heflin & Alaimo, 2007, p. 172). These skills are tracked to measure success and are then measured to gauge the abilities of students to generalize the discrete behaviors into appropriate contexts.

As students get older and/or master more skills, they not only generalize these skills, they also learn that behaviors reap positive and negative consequences. This paradigm has been controversial. Many opponents of ABA believe that the learned DTT behavior detracts from cognition and creativity. Music educators should understand that when working with students who have autism, the use of a consistent behavior program across campus and in all school situations, is critical to success. ABA can be very effective when applied correctly and consistently across the curriculum. Much of what is suggested later in this chapter is based on this paradigm and the use of positive reinforcement.

Because of the training that special educators receive, they may be inclined to isolate specific behavior using positive reinforcement. This is common in special education and education psychology training. When ABA strategies are used correctly, they work. However, it is important for music teachers to look at all the methods discussed in this chapter to encourage positive behavior with students on the autism spectrum.

The best outcome occurs when adults realize and successfully implement the most appropriate behavior method for a particular student. For this reason, knowledge of and experience in all methods is advantageous.

OUTBURSTS, MELTDOWNS, AND OTHER DISRUPTIONS

The terms "outburst," "tantrum," and "meltdown" are familiar to most teachers. Regardless of which term is used, teachers who work with students on the autism spectrum understand what is being said and may have experienced the behavior with students in their classrooms. After such an event, the appropriate first step in curbing this behavior is to get together with other faculty and staff to address what happened. However, when working together on a behavior issue, education professionals sometimes neglect to remember that the "behavior issue" is attached to a child and that there are often extenuating circumstances involved, especially with a child on the spectrum. It is important to refer to these occurrences in the most positive light possible. Moreover, sometimes a child is just being a child and the behavior has nothing to do with the label.

To reframe the deficit or negative paradigm, it is often helpful to imagine living in a world where fear and anxiety can come at anytime. In this world, anxiety is central to everyday life, and the entire day is focused on trying to identify, avoid, or cope with these strong and persistent feelings. In addition, there is often little or no ability to communicate feelings to others or to understand your own emotions or the emotions of those around you. It is obvious that this would be a very uncomfortable, frustrating, and difficult way to live, and it is usually an important factor in the occurrence of meltdowns. The intent of the behavior is not to disrupt the day of the teacher or other students. The student with autism is conveying a need, fear, anxiety, and/or frustration.

This anxiety is central to the life for students who struggle with autism. For them, every day can be like this. Life is a constant battle of fear, anxiety, and frustration. When a child on the autism spectrum does have that meltdown, outburst, or tantrum, it is a signal to his teacher. A student may be attempting to express his fears or anxieties, and that he needs assistance adjusting to the teaching environment. Rarely do students have these meltdowns to intentionally disrupt a lesson. To do this would require a better grasp of theory of mind than most students with autism, who have disparate communication skills, are able to display. These behavioral outbursts are forms of communication and function as an indication that something is amiss in the student's environment.

The Antecedent

Understanding the antecedent to a meltdown is an important key to altering behaviors that are inappropriate. Did a random loud noise occur in your room the day before? Are there florescent lights in the room that bother the student? How were things going for this student earlier in the school day? Often, examining these precursors can assist when adapting the learning environment for a student with autism. Figure 5.1 is a tool to assist in assessing and collecting data regarding a behavior that disrupts the music classroom.

After determining the totality of the student's day and how it may have affected his behavior, music teachers are encouraged to strategize with other educators in the building to communicate regarding any events or challenges that may cause a further issue later in the day. For example, a classroom teacher may share that there was a guest speaker in class. This changed the class schedule for the day, and Mark is having difficulty coping with these changes. These communications are very helpful for a music teacher who, in turn, may then have a greater understanding of future behavior disruptions in a music classroom.

The Behavior

It is also paramount to examine the behavior itself and ask what was the intent of the outburst. Was it meant to communicate something to you, a staff member, or another student? For example, many children on the spectrum cannot express to another person when they are feeling unwell (have a cold, etc.). An outburst may just be an expression of discomfort.

Behavior Assessment		
Antecedent	Behavior	Consequence
Notes:		

Figure 5.1
Behavior Assessment
Source: Adapted from Hodgdon, 1999, p. 70

CAUTIONARY CONSIDERATIONS

- Do not label a behavior "bad" without understanding the intent of the behavior. If a child continues to hear that she is "bad," it will have a negative affect on her self-esteem.
- Do not assume that students with autism will understand the procedures and social expectations in an active music classroom or ensemble. They must be laid out explicitly to the student and often written down on paper. Also, a behavior plan may not work for all students with autism.
- Do not intercede to extinguish a behavior until you understand why a student is engaging in that behavior.

A meltdown may also indicate that an event that will happen soon is causing a student anxiety. For example, the end of a school day is a difficult transition for many students with autism. They may be anxious about going home. All behaviors have intent. It is important to also examine intent as well as cause.

The Consequence

Finally, it is imperative to examine the consequence of a behavior. This is especially critical if it is a behavior not desired by the teacher. Sometimes, students are looking for attention. If the student is getting a certain pleasing or stimulating reaction from a teacher, he will repeat the behavior. He may continue to repeat the behavior to witness what effect it has on the teacher or his classmates. In these cases, and this can be difficult (especially if it is scream or an outburst), it is important to ignore the student. This may require other students to ignore the behavior as well. This may be difficult for students, especially if the behavior is loud or disruptive. Consult your special education team for support and assistance. It is important to understand that a behavior that is ignored will often increase in frequency and magnitude prior to slowly fading.

ODD OR REPETITIVE BEHAVIOR

Music educators sometimes experience students with autism engaging in odd, unusual, or repetitive behaviors, known as "stimming." These are often done for self-stimulation. As an example, Adam may continuously look at a wind chime in the music room. He may enjoy viewing it from many angles.

Adam may push the wind chime and then walk around it repeatedly as he views the light shining through it. This type of behavior is common in children with autism. The self-pleasing that Adam experiences may also serve to calm his frustrations and anxieties, and provide a momentary haven of relaxation during his day.

The difficulty increases when the teacher attempts to engage the student. Adam may not want to join the class for music. He would rather look at the wind chimes. Many professionals who work with children on the autism spectrum explain stimming as a form of self-imposed isolation. As mentioned in previous chapters, some students with autism would rather be in the comfort of their own private world than in the world around them. The world of the wind chimes may make much more sense to Adam than the recorders and folk dancing planned for music class that day.

Getting Adam to engage in music class may take awhile. It may require finding something he really enjoys. Adam may be able to transfer his interest in wind chimes to the glockenspiel or finger cymbals. It may be useful to use the wind chimes as a reward for participating in music class. Whatever strategy is chosen, it is important to understand that allowing a child to recuse himself from interacting with his peers is not always positive or advised. Students with autism must interact with the world around them in order to learn. Isolated and inward behavior is not conducive for learning. However, sometimes it can be entirely appropriate to allow a student to engage in his preferred behavior for a limited period of time. This is particularly important when a student needs a break from instruction or is temporarily overstimulated during class. Almost everyone becomes overstimulated at some point in time. Considering the amount of stimulation students in school experience, a break may be a welcome respite before students reenter the world of songs and games.

BEHAVIOR AND COMMUNICATION

When working with students on the spectrum, a consistent finding is that behavior and communication are inherently linked. Often students with autism, because of their communication challenges, express behaviors that are also attempts to communicate needs. Hodgdon (1999) states: "Behavior and communication are intertwined. It is important to understand that these students communicate differently. What they understand and how they attempt to communicate with others may not be what is typical for their peers" (p. 59). Figure 5.2 shows some examples of behaviors linked to communication.

1. Causing pain to others to express their pain
2. Uncomfortable with learning environment. May cause disruption to be moved away
3. Repeating verbal cues for self-stimulation
4. Inappropriate touching to initiate play
5. Cognitive processing delays

Figure 5.2
Examples of Behaviors Linked to Communication

When assessing these behaviors, consider a few distinct potential causes and possible intentions for the behavior:

1. I do not understand (receptive-language interruption).
   Example: Joseph doesn't understand that you are telling him he cannot play the drums.
2. I am not comfortable.
   Example: Joseph does not like the loud noises in your room. The florescent lights in your room also distract Joseph.
3. I cannot express myself.
   Example: Joseph is not feeling well today and has trouble expressing his discomfort.
4. I do not Feel I have any control (which is akin to feeling unsafe).
   Example: The routine has been interrupted because of an all-school assembly. Events are not happening in the appropriate order.

As we stated in chapter 3, there are many nuances in what a student communicates. The more familiar a teacher is with a student, the easier it is to understand his unique characteristics. This, in turn, will allow for fewer behavior challenges based on communication. In addition, the more effective a teacher is when communicating with a student with autism, the less often meltdowns based on communication difficulties will occur. When trust has been achieved in a student/teacher relationship, frustration and anxiety will be greatly alleviated.

SCHEDULE, ROUTINE, AND THE LINK WITH BEHAVIOR

Interruptions in a schedule or routine often cause disruptive behaviors in students with autism. Many teachers often misread behaviors that are associated with these disruptions. Students with autism experience high anxiety regarding events in their lives they cannot control. A defined schedule allows the student to understand and anticipate the happenings in his life. Schedules can be written (if the student can read) or can be created using icons. Figures 5.3 and 5.4 are examples of a picture schedule.

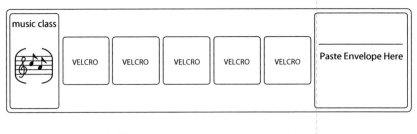

Use Boardmaker™ to place Picutre Communication Symbols© here.

Figure 5.3
Music Class. PECS schedule constructed on Boardmaker
Suggested use: Put title, symbol representing the activity, individual's name, or individual's picture in the first cell. Laminate sheet and attach the cells above with Velcro. As each task is completed, remove the corresponding symbol and place it in the envelope.
Source: The Picture Communications Symbols ©1981–2011 by Mayer-Johnson LLC. All Rights Reserved Worldwide. Used with permission. Boardmaker® is a trademark of Mayer-Johnston LLC.

The picture icons on these schedules are from Boardmaker. Many school systems own this program.

School events that are seen as rewards by the schoolwide community can function as stress-induced negative instances for students with autism. As an example, an elementary school had been rewarded for achieving a high standard of physical fitness by having a professional team of dancers and singers come present a dance party for the students. The school was literally buzzing with excitement as the younger students began to enter the gymnasium for the dance party. As the loud music began, a first-grade boy named Timmy put his hands over his ears and bumped his head into the side of his teacher. He was clearly in distress. The teacher pointed to the back of the gym and told him to go sit there as the rest of the students and teachers began dancing and singing. Timmy walked to the back of the gym, rolled into a ball, and rocked back and forth with his hands over his ears. He began moaning and crying as the school dance party continued. Finally, the music teacher saw him, let the first-grade teacher know she was going to take him with her, and walked him out of the gym.

This seemingly positive school event was a very negative experience for this student. Planning ahead, using a calendar and schedule, and having a plan B in case some students became anxious may have helped create a much more positive experience for Timmy. Much of the stress and anxiety created in schools can be traced to disruptions in schedule, lack of planning,

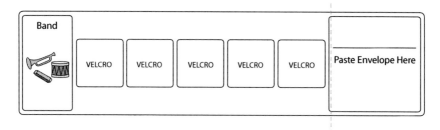

Use Boardmaker™ to place Picutre Communication Symbols© here.

Figure 5.4
Band. PECS schedule constructed on Boardmaker
Suggested use: Put title, symbol representing the activity, individual's name, or individual's picture in the first cell. Laminate sheet and attach cells above with Velcro. As each task is completed, remove the corresponding symbol and place it in the envelope. Use Boardmaker to place Picture Communication Symbols here.
Source: The Picture Communications Symbols ©1981–2011 by Mayer-Johnson LLC. All Rights Reserved Worldwide. Used with permission. Boardmaker® is a trademark of Mayer-Johnston LLC.

and infrequent communication between school staff and between the adults and students who work together in a school community.

Students with autism may carry a notebook with pre-made icons in place. These icons can be arranged to represent the order of the activities in a music lesson or ensemble rehearsal. This particular schedule shown in figure 5.3 is for a general music classroom and a band rehearsal. A student places icons on the schedule according to the music class schedule. Velcro is used to attach the pictures. After the event is over, the student places the icons in the envelope, signifying that the event is finished and the next event is ready to begin. A student may also carry dividers for each class within a 3-ring binder. A paraprofessional can arrange icons according to the schedule provided by each teacher. This assists students with autism in predicting their day and decreases anxiety regarding the expectations and activities of each portion of the day. Figure 5.4 is an example for an older student attending a band class.

A disruption in a schedule can make a student with autism uncomfortable and anxious. Teachers can reduce these occurrences (e.g., meltdowns) by priming the student for the changes in the schedule far in advance. This may include showing her pictures of the event, creating social stories about what will happen at the event (see chapter 3), and using other reinforcers to assist with communication. As an example, if a music teacher is having a concert in the auditorium, he may need to prepare a student with autism by taking him to the auditorium ahead of time. The teacher may take a picture of the audience to show the student and have a microphone set up so the student will know the potential volume. Furthermore, the teacher may allow the student to attend similar concerts in the auditorium so he can experience what it is like during a performance. Obviously, this should be done in consultation with the special education team and perhaps the parents. There are many extra steps that can be taken to make a concert run smoothly for a student with autism. This preparation creates a more positive and meaningful experience for all students (and parents). These techniques may also have assisted Timmy in preparation for the dance party (as would have a pair of headphones to dampen the sound and sunglasses for the visual stimuli).

Behaviors connected to changes in schedules can also be about loss of control. Students with autism often feel most comfortable when life is predictable and controllable. Music teachers may transition into these changes by allowing the student to control the classroom schedule. For example, if there are four activities or segments of class that day, the music teacher may allow the student with autism to choose the order of the segments. After the student becomes more comfortable, the music teacher may consider fading this option as new options and behaviors are chosen and shaped.

Social stories are another way to prepare a student with autism for a change or significant event. These were discussed at length in chapter 3 (see figure 3.3). In that example, the expected behaviors are addressed. For example, Spencer is told where to sit, where to hang up his coat, and so forth. These expectations can be generalized to significant events such as a field trip or a concert.

Students with autism also need to learn to regulate themselves when changes do occur. Change is a part of life. Therefore, music teachers should not be afraid to change schedules and routines. The key is to not make changes without warning. Prime the student for changes in schedule early by discussing them, and by using pictures and social stories to help the student with autism understand what will happen. Consult with the special education team to find the most clear and consistent way to do so. Learning how a student is introduced to change in other areas of the building will provide information to help accomplish the same task in music.

CAUTIONARY CONSIDERATIONS

- Do not underestimate the effect a change in schedule or sensory input can have on the behavior of a student with autism. Change can be traumatic for a child with autism and often leads to outward behavior.
- Prepare the student for change as far in advance as possible with pictures and other communication that the student understands. This will help with the transitions and behaviors associated with these transitions.

CREATING A BEHAVIOR PLAN FOR A STUDENT WITH AUTISM

The first priority after a behavior manifests itself is to determine whether it is indeed a problem behavior (or, who has the problem—student or teacher), and to examine the intent of the behavior. The role of a teacher is to consult with the special education team (including the IEP document) to see which, if any, of these issues are noted as goals for the student and how those behavioral issues relate to the behaviors the music teacher has observed in the classroom or ensemble. The music teacher may need assistance from special education professionals to determine the types and intent of specific behaviors. For example, if an outburst is experienced during instruction, one of the first strategies is to consult the special education team and IEP to find out what steps are being used in other classes to curb the student's impulse-control issues.

It is also helpful to take data regarding the outburst or episode. Noting any possible antecedents to the behavior (what was happening just before the student exhibited the negative behavior), or timing the length of the disruption, can be powerful tools for determining cause and effect. By examining paperwork, taking data, and consulting the special education team, a music teacher can create a plan and adapt behavior expectations accordingly.

Figure 5.5 outlines potential challenging behaviors in the music classroom. Many students with autism may exhibit behaviors that appear in Figure 5.5 but have completely different intentions than those that might be expected. For example, a student may cause harm to another student to show everyone that he does not feel well or is experiencing pain himself. Because of his communication and cognition delays, this may be the only way for him to express himself.

Whether a behavior is intentional or not, the learning of all students must be protected. Students with autism often respond best to concrete plans that have direct and meaningful consequences to actions. Often, teachers make mistakes by making rules that are complicated and abstract.

1. Cause injury or harm to others
2. Causes injury or harm to themselves
3. Disrupts the learning of others in the music classroom
4. Not age appropriate
5. Does not comply with the rules of school or the music classroom
6. Seeks attention
7. The behavior is a substitute for appropriate means of communication

Figure 5.5
Examples of Problem or Concerning Behaviors

Create rules that are simple and few, and outline direct and meaningful consequences for breaking the rules.

Many teachers have found success by creating a personal-behavior plan for a student who is struggling in a music classroom. These plans are grounded in positive reinforcement; students earn privileges for behaving appropriately, and inappropriate behavior has concrete consequences.

The first step in establishing a personal-behavior plan is to determine the types of activities or items that a student loves. It may be to play a drum, lead other students in an activity, or use the computer. This may require some exploratory time and may require consultation with the special education team and parents. Ultimately, every student will work for something or some reward. The interesting challenge when working with students who do not always communicate in a way we can understand is to determine the items, activities, and rewards that will function best for a student with autism.

Once the reward items have been established, there are several ways to implement a personal-behavior plan. Figure 5.6 shows a level system that allows student to move up or down based on appropriate or inappropriate behaviors. This can be something that he keeps in a separate notebook and, when in class, a teacher can ask to see the notebook if a level change is needed.

Figure 5.6 is obviously for higher-functioning students (those who are able to read). It can be adapted based on the current ability level of any student (e.g., use picture icons instead of words). Figure 5.6 can also be used in all the student's classes. Students can move up or down based on broader behavior goals. For example, a student who is having trouble following directions and participating correctly in music may have the same issues in other classes. A consistent behavior plan has been shown to have the most success.

Level 4	Level 3	Level 2	Level 1
Can have choice time with drums, computer, or music books	Can have chice with drums or music books	Can have choice time with music books	No choice time

I can move up by:
1. participating in music class in a positive way
2. answering questions
3. following directions

I can move down by:
1. not participating in music class
2. interrupting the learning of others
3. not following directions

Figure 5.6
Personal-Behavior Level System

Found my book	☐
Sat in my seat	☐
Followed directions	☐
Kept my hands to myself	☐

Figure 5.7
Personal-Behavior Checklist

Figure 5.7 is designed to promote concrete behavior. These behaviors can assist students as they understand exactly what is expected. Pictures (e.g., Boardmaker icons) can be used as well to highlight these steps with students who cannot read, write, or who are nonverbal.

The personal-behavior checklist can be modified to fit any student. In this case, the student did not keep his hands to himself. This may mean he does not earn a privilege or it may affect his participation grade in a particular class. Make everything that is expected of a student with autism as concrete as possible. Specific parameters can be removed after these positive behaviors become routine or reintroduced if there is a recurring or returning issue.

SOCIAL SKILLS AND BEHAVIOR

It is crucial to consider social skills when examining behavior. Socialization strategies will be examined in depth in chapter 6. However, social skill development can have a profound affect on behavior. Students with autism can be socially awkward, introverted, or exhibit social behavior that is not characteristic of their chronological age. This may cause other students to react in a negative way to students with autism. Vignette 5.2 is an example of such a situation.

When an instance similar to the one described in vignette 5.2 occurs, it is important to teach both Mark and Jason appropriate responses to this type

---

Vignette 5.2
MARK AND JASON

Both Mark and Jason are walking down the hallway in front of Ms. Karon's choir room. Ms. Karen sees that Mark is attempting to discuss all of the details of a Sesame Street video that he watches at home. Jason is rolling his eyes and ignoring Mark. Finally, Jason says to Mark: "Sesame Street is for babies!" Mark is visibly upset by the interaction.

Discussion:

How would you encourage appropriate behavior for both Jason and Mark?

1. Anxiety disorders
2. ADHD
3. Depression
4. Mood Disorders (depression, bipolar, obsessive compulsive)
5. Sleep disorders
6. Nutrition deficits

Figure 5.8
Potential Medical Issues for Children with Autism
Source: Hodgdon, 1999.

of interaction. Mark must learn the appropriate social behavior in this situation. Clearly, he has trouble relating to age-appropriate activities and should not "hound" Jason about the details of the video. Jason should learn to be accepting of differences among his peers and be more patient. This event happened in the hallway but could just as easily occurred in a classroom. The goal is to teach acceptance and appropriate social behavior.

RELATED MEDICAL ISSUES AND BEHAVIOR

For anyone, health can relate to behavior. A child who is not feeling well will not want to participate in school. Children with autism typically have related health issues that may affect how they behave in school. Many issues are individualized to a student. Figure 5.8 presents examples of related health issues for students on the spectrum.

Music teachers find value in considering these medical challenges as separate but related issues. For example, if Adam has a sleep disorder associated with his autism, he may come to class exhausted and may need special considerations. This information may or may not be in his IEP.

This all relates to the idea that students on the spectrum have a difficult time expressing themselves. If a child is not feeling well, he will inevitably have a difficult time learning in music class. Continued communication with the special education staff and parents regarding these medical concerns will assist in the overall understanding of the child and his experiences (positive and negative) during the school day.

CONCLUSION: ASSESSMENT OF BEHAVIOR (TAKING DATA FOR THE IEP)

We advocate that the appropriate placement of students with special needs is imperative to success for everyone in the music classroom or ensemble. Often, behavior in class can be a signal that the placement is overwhelming for a student with autism. In addition, this data may also be key in advocating for appropriate support and services in the music classroom. For example, if Bruce's meltdown lasted 10 minutes and instruction in choir was lost during that episode, Bruce's classmates did not receive instruction during that time, either. This behavior manifestation, then, becomes an issue for everyone in the room.

Document *any* behavior that disrupts learning for the students in your classroom with the understanding that these behaviors are expressions of autism and are not necessarily a sign that a student intends to interrupt learning. Therefore, if difficult behaviors persist, music teachers are advised to alert the team, put new behavior interventions in place, attempt to increase communication avenues between the teacher and the student, attend or send information to IEP meetings, and to tirelessly advocate for appropriate placement if students are in learning environments that are deleterious to their musical education and well-being. It is the goal of music education to teach all students. The placement of a student within a different classroom, at a different time of day, with a different group of students, or on a different day of the week, can make a difference as well. The more data that can be taken, and the more proactive a music educator can be in advocating for the appropriate placement of all students (those with and without autism), the closer the goal of providing a music education for all students will be.

It is also important to analyze behaviors in a way that is not personal. Students with autism do not have a vendetta. They often lack the tools necessary to behave appropriately. Break down disruptive behaviors and retrace the child's day. Have many conversations with other faculty, staff, and parents to get to the cause of the behavior.

Also consider self-esteem. Students with autism can hear that they are "bad" very often. Imagine hearing this from an adult for years and years without the opportunity to defend or state your case. Encourage good behavior, and let students know when they do something *right* or *good*. This is imperative in teaching the whole child.

REFERENCES

Baer, D. M., Wolf, M. M., & Risely, T. (1968). Current dimensions of applied behavior analysis. *Journal of Applied Behavior Analysis, 20,* 313–328.

Hammel, A. M. (1999). *A study of teacher competencies necessary when including special learners in elementary music classrooms: The development of a unit of study for use with undergraduate music education students.* DMA dissertation, Shenandoah University (AAT 9926079).

Heflin, L. J., & Alaimo, D. F. (2007). *Students with autism spectrum disorders.* Upper Saddle River, NJ: Pearson.

Hodgdon, L. A. (1999). *Solving behavior problems in autism: Improving communication with visual strategies.* Troy, MI; QuirkRoberts Publishing.

DISCUSSION QUESTIONS

1. Think of any child you have been in contact with who has been diagnosed with autism. How does communication affect his behavior?
2. Have you seen behavior plans instituted in music classrooms? Explain.
3. What kinds of strategies do you use to encourage appropriate behavior in your classroom? How can these strategies be adapted for a student with autism?

CHAPTER 6

Understanding the Socialization of Students with Autism Spectrum Disorder

---

CHAPTER OVERVIEW

Students with autism often are challenged in the area of social skills and social development. This chapter highlights the following areas of concern for students with autism in the music classroom:

- The fundamentals of social development
- Socialization strategies in the music classroom
- Strategies for extending joint attention and eye contact in the music classroom
- Peer relationships and affective development
- Reverse inclusion

Persons with autism typically have deficits in many areas of social development. In fact, many researchers consider socialization challenges to be the hallmark of autism (Kanner, 1943). Beginning at birth, infants with autism may not show interest in objects or people, may not play simple interaction games, or laugh or smile in response to positive statements (Carter, Davis, Klin, & Volkmar, 2005). As children with autism get older, they may have limited interest in social speech, imitation, and joint attention that culminates in a lack of social function or understanding of social cues. Theimann and Goldstein (2001) state: "This limited repertoire of social communication behaviors may interfere with academic progress *and* friendship development" (p. 425).

Vignette 6.1
DOUG

Doug is in his first day of orchestra. After much consideration, he has decided to learn violin. Doug comes to class, sits down, and waits for Ms. Hudzik to begin teaching. There are about eight new violinists in class sitting next to him. Ms. Hudzik begins by telling the students to open their cases and take out their bows, being careful not to touch the hair on the bow.

Ms. Hudzik then begins to show the students how to hold the bow. "Thumb near the frog, fingers resting on top, and pinky finger on the screw," she says as she holds the bow up for the students to see. Doug doesn't look up at Ms. Huszik as she models holding the bow. The other students are watching each other as they attempt to imitate Ms. Huszik. Doug continues to stare down at the bow having no idea where to begin. He does not look to his peers for clues and gets frustrated when being helped by his friends.

Ms. Hudzik noticed that Doug did not come to the next class. When she inquired about it, his classroom teacher explained that Doug did not want to do orchestra anymore.

Discussion:
- Why did Doug really decide to not continue orchestra?
- What are the bigger-picture concerns for Doug if he does not return to orchestra?
- What could Ms. Hudzik do to help Doug imitate her in orchestra class?

Social communication and academic progress are inherently linked. In fact, Bandura (1977) goes one step further and explains that social learning is at the crux of the human learning experience and that observing and modeling others is the primary way humans learn. She explains that we learn by observing the behaviors of others as well as from the outcomes of those behaviors (p. 440). This lack of or difference in social communication can present difficulties for music teachers. Learning, especially in music, is a social experience. Making music together is an integral part of the goal of music education at all levels. Especially in music learning, a student or a teacher modeling the appropriate way to hold a bow or buzz into a mouthpiece is an intricate part of a music lesson.

Teachers interested in teaching the whole child, not just a music curriculum, appreciate that most of what we examine in this chapter can be generalized to all children and is not limited to those with autism. Any child, with or without autism, may have imitation, joint-attention, and socialization issues that create obstacles to their learning and in their ability to create relationships. This chapter sequences socialization challenges for students with autism in the music classroom and offers broad, cohesive strategies for creating an inviting social atmosphere for students with autism.

THE FUNDAMENTALS OF SOCIAL DEVELOPMENT AND CHILDREN WITH AUTISM

Before looking into a school-aged child with autism and his social development, music teachers should first consider how a typical child develops before entering school and how this may differ for a child with autism. Many students with autism are either developing these fundamentals or have not encountered opportunities to practice these basic social skills enough to become a part of the socialization within the classroom (e.g., social speech and collaborative play). Specifically, this chapter examines the following pillars of social development in students with autism: eye contact and joint attention, social speech and social play, affective development, imitation, and peer relationships and social interaction. In addition, we provide specific strategies for adapting lessons and creating an appropriate social musical learning environment.

Gaze/Eye Contact, Joint Attention, and Socialization

Eye gaze and joint attention have been discussed at length in other chapters as they apply to communication and cognition. Eye gaze and joint attention also challenge the ability of a child with autism to be social. For a child with autism, this usually starts at birth. Typically, infants come into the world already "hardwired" to begin social relationships with their parents and other caregivers (Carter et al., 2005). Through eye gaze and joint attention, they show preferences for people, objects, food, and other things that give them pleasure. In fact, these are the beginnings of dialogue between mother and infant. Carter and colleagues state: "This nonverbal facial 'dialogue' between infant and caregiver provides the context for very early socialization, providing critical opportunities for learning" (p. 318).

As individuals with autism get older, they may continue to find the human face and emotional intent confusing. In fact, persons with autism often avoid eye contact. However, eye contact can be a very powerful form of social communication. Through rehearsal (in therapy), a student with autism will learn to make eye contact; yet, the meaning of the expression on a face may remain confusing to her. Teachers may need to explain emotions to a student with autism, even though they seem to be clearly written all over the face.

Extending Eye Contact and Joint Attention in the Music Classroom

Extending eye contact is important in working with students on the autism spectrum. This includes eye contact with the teacher and with other students in the classroom. In simple day-to-day interactions, insist on appropriate eye contact. In a band classroom, this type of eye contact can be rehearsed as a global skill that all students are mastering. All band students are encouraged to watch the conductor and make eye contact whenever possible. By creating a universal goal, everyone (all students, rather than just the student with autism) can benefit from the same set of expectations.

In an elementary classroom, eye contact can be included in the sequence of steps in a folk dance. One of the first skills students learn is to look their partner in the eye and say, "May I have this dance?" Eye contact is considered universally appropriate and is especially good for students with autism. When students perform the folk dance steps in sequence because it allows students to begin to feel the community culture that is built through these authentic experiences. One transferrable goal is that a student will be able to go to a local folk-dance evening and join in the experience with others.

In chapter 1 we provided an overview of various therapies used to treat autism. One strategy is Floortime/DIR. The basic principle of Floortime is to follow the child's lead when developing her social and communication skills. This is a place where special education, music therapy and music education often intersect. From the perspective of a music educator, it may mean following the child's lead to determine the music he likes and what skills he has mastered, as well as the types of music and activities that keep his interest. Figures 6.1 and 6.2 are examples of Floortime-based lesson plans for the music classroom.

Figures 6.1 and 6.2 have a goal to extend joint attention to music. This strategy expands to include the engagement of a student with autism throughout his musical life. The long-term strategy is to increase the length and depth of joint attention, reciprocation, and engagement. The signs of improvement are often subtle and teachers track minutes (seconds) of engagement and work to expand accordingly. This may also be accomplished in an included small-group percussion lesson by taking turns with students who want to lead the group. Figure 6.2 is an example of a Floortime-inspired general music lesson. Vignette 6.2 is an example of how a student with autism may think and feel after experiencing that lesson.

When working with a student who has autism in the music classroom, expanding joint attention and making eye contact may be the most important additions to a socialization-teaching skill set. Not only does this

---

6th Grade Band

Percussion

Objective:

1. Student will be able to perform eighth notes in any combination on any beat using duple meter.
2. Extend engagement, joint attention, and eye gaze

Materials and Set up:

1. Practice pads set up so that teacher (or a coached, peer helper) and student can face each other.
2. Two (or more) pairs of snare drum sticks (no music at the outset)

Procedure:

1. Teacher will begin by allowing a student to explore rhythms on the practice pad by playing whatever duple meter combinations he or she wants.
   a. If students are challenged with no. 1, they could say rhythm patterns.
   b. Students can take turns being the leader of the group.
2. Percussion section will echo the duple pattern that the student leader plays.
3. Teacher will listen to see if there are any patterns that can be used in the lesson to further their understanding of duple meter (that the student is playing or saying).
4. If there are no recognizable patterns, the teacher will play a simple eighth-note pattern for the students to echo. Teacher will make eye contact when possible.
5. If there is a suitable duple pattern, the teacher will echo the pattern back to the student. Repeat three times.
6. The teacher then plays a similar pattern for the student to echo on the practice pad.
7. After the student echoes a pattern on the practice pad correctly, teacher will attempt to move to a different duple meter pattern.
8. As the student masters each pattern aurally, the teacher will point to the music as she is performing the pattern and allow the student to point.
9. Teacher will attempt to extend the pattern echoing back and forth throughout the lesson.
10. Repeat steps 2 through 8. Can be used to introduce meters, rhythms, syncopation, notation, etc.

Assessment Strategies

1. Keep track of the number of reciprocations back and forth between the teacher and student and track over time. The teacher will then build longer musical engagement strategies into the next lesson to extend joint attention.
2. Assess mastery of duple rhythm skills in different combinations.

Figure 6.1
Floortime-Based Lesson (Band/Orch)

technique assist a student with future music learning, it also helps students with autism transfer the social skills they have learned to experiences in other classes and in their socialization with peers.

Social Speech and Social Play

As discussed in chapter 3, one cornerstone of autism is a delay in communication skills. Many persons with autism have substantial communication

---

Elementary General Music Class

Objectives: Students will demonstrate competence in creating, verbalizing, and performing ostinati using quarter, paired eighth, half, and sixteenth notes (and the corresponding rests).

Adapted Objective (for David): David will extend his joint attention to music (rhythm ostinato) from 5 minutes to 7 minutes.

Essential questions (for the students):

1. What is the term for a repeated rhythmic pattern in music?
2. How can we create these patterns?
3. In what ways can we apply ostinati to songs and games?

Procedures:

1. Students will respond to essential questions and begin to improvise by creating ostinati that are four beats in length.
2. Students will identify the rhythmic elements used in their ostinati by using rhythm syllables and associating them to rhythms found in Ida Red.
3. Class will sing and play Ida Red while individual students perform ostinati patterns.

Accommodations for David:

1. Student chosen to perform ostinati patterns will have the time and tempo adjusted. He will be able to practice his ostinato and perform it while the class sings and plays the Ida Red game.
2. David will not be asked to verbalize his pattern. He will be given time to program the pattern into his assistive technology with his paraprofessional. This student may present his patterns to me prior to the next music class.

Assessment: Students will be assessed on their ability to create an ostinato pattern, verbalize the pattern using rhythm syllables, and will experience/perform the patterns in isolation and as part of a game.

Figure 6.2
Floortime-Inspired Lesson Plan for a Third-Grade Inclusion

challenges. However, they also exhibit *social* communication challenges from birth that continue to be evident throughout their lives. Infants with autism show lower preferences than typically developing children for listening to speech and lack preverbal vocalizations before they learn to talk (Sheinkopf, Mundy, Oller, & Steffens, 2000). As they get older, these challenges continue because children with autism do not "initiate and integrate the basic interpersonal patterns that are believed to be the foundation for all later communication" (Carter et al., 2005). This challenges their ability to form lasting social relationships.

The bigger issue for children on the spectrum is their *interest* in social speech. The further a child is removed from the social vernacular of peers, the less often he will attempt to engage them. This begins a never-ending spiral that can result in the typical introversion seen in students with autism. As they get older, the gap between these students and their peers' social

---

Vignette 6.2
DAVID

David had been waiting for weeks to hear his teacher talk about "ostinati" again. He loved creating his own ostinato patterns at home and had been practicing them with his mom. He got very excited when he heard that his teacher would be working on creating ostinati again in music class. David preprogrammed his adaptive assisted technology to say "ostinato" to respond to the teacher's predictable question—"who can tell me the name of a pattern that repeats many times in music?"—he was ready!

David was more than ready for ostinato day in music class. His teacher was very impressed with his almost immediate response to her question, and David was the first student to perform an ostinato pattern on the rug of the music classroom. The other students responded by copying David's pattern, and soon the class was engaged in creating and repeating patterns for each other. David was doing very well until he became lost in the quick repetitions and performances of new rhythmic ideas. This could have been the start to a bad experience for David and his classmates. Fortunately, his music teacher was aware of the issue and was able to have the classmates follow David's lead in creating and repeating ostinato patterns. The class began singing "Ida Red" and David led the class in ostinati performances as they sang and played the game. It was a beautiful, organic experience within this third-grade general music classroom.

With the assistance of his paraprofessional, David was able to understand what was happening. He finished the class in a positive way and was looking forward to the next time he could "shine" in music class.

---

speech increases, leaving them out of the social fold of their own daily lives. For example, as mentioned in chapter 3, students with autism engage in echolalia (repeated speech patterns). Other students may not understand this behavior and, instead of trying to problem solve, will choose not to interact with them. This is just one of many ways social speech can interrupt a child's ability to form relationships.

Students who are higher functioning may need to be taught the basic slang or jokes their peers use in the lunchroom or the hallways in a very literal way. They may be afraid to join in because it confuses them. The student with autism also may not know the best response if a peer is trying to be friendly to him by telling a joke. It is okay to label figures of speech, jokes, references, and other things if a student needs a frame of reference for them. For example, when entering the music classroom he may hear all the students saying, "What's up?" Some students with autism might literally look up at the ceiling if they have never heard that phrase before (or if what it means has not been explained to them). Another example might be that he hears a student say, "I'm going to kill her!" A teacher may need to explain that this is a figure of speech and that the student who said it really means that he is upset or unhappy with his friend, and that he is not going to hurt anyone.

When it comes to social play, children typically move from the manipulation of objects through parallel play and the appropriate use of toys (e.g., feeding a doll or placing trains on the tracks in a logical line) into social play (Carter et al., 2005). Children with autism, however, usually develop much differently. They may be interested in objects because of an ability to manipulate them in a stereotypical way rather than their functional or symbolic use. For example, a child with autism may be interested in a dump truck because he thinks the wheels spin in an interesting way. A neurotypical child, while interested in the spinning wheels, will also be interested in using the truck to dump sand from the sand box and in creating new uses for the dump truck. The interruption in the social interaction between two children playing with the same truck is obvious.

Social Speech and Social Play in the Music Classroom

The same two young students may find themselves in music class together. A common beat-passing chant is "Engine Engine Number Nine":

> *Engine engine number nine*
> *going down Chicago line.*
> *If the train falls off the track,*
> *do I get my money back?*
> *Yes. No. Maybe so.*

The music teacher may decide to use trains as beat-passing devices and have students work in pairs to pass the train back and forth to the beat. The student with autism may initially have difficulty with the natural give and take of this activity; however, the social gains, paired with the gains in musical competency, are well worth the time it may take to teach this behavior. Through modeling, chunking (breaking the beat-passing motions into small parts), and repeated practice, students with autism can be taught to pass the truck on the beat and to make eye contact while doing so. Finally, once this behavior is taught, it can be transferred and generalized to other situations.

CAUTIONARY CONSIDERATIONS

- Do not forget to consider universal design for learning (UDL) when planning interventions and expectations for students with autism. The specific principles of UDL can be found at http://www.udlcenter.org.
- Some students do not automatically engage in social conversations and behaviors with a student who has autism. These experiences may need to be carefully structured and sequenced. Anything you can do to facilitate social engagement can be of great help to a student with autism. Social games and activities can serve as a vehicle as well as help all students engage with the content.

Affective Development

"Affective development" is a term used to describe the ways in which we advance our understanding of emotions. This includes understanding our own emotions as well as the emotional intentions of others. In the first three years of life, children learn to recognize and label their own emotional states, as well as those of others (Carter et al., 2005). Students with autism tend to have difficulty with both endeavors. In particular, they have difficulty interpreting facial expressions that include emotion. Teachers sometimes must literally explain the emotion on their faces when students with autism are unable to read them. For example, a student may ask his teacher whether another child is "happy crying or sad crying." The teacher may then need to explain that the child is crying, not because he is happy, but because he is sad that he didn't get a turn in class. Frequent concrete encounters like this can eventually lead a student on the spectrum to a greater understanding of facial expressions and emotion. In addition, having students with autism understand their own emotions as well as the emotions of their peers is crucial to their overall social development. In music, this is an essential component within our curriculum that can be adapted to provide meaningful social-learning experiences for all students. This is, after all, one of the basic tenets of inclusion.

Affective Development in the Music Classroom

A well-known song taught to a sol-mi-do pattern is often used in elementary music classrooms, "Billy Sad":

SS	M	SS	M	SS	MM	SS	M
Billy	sad.	Billy	sad.	Tell me	why are	you so	sad?
SS	M	SS	MM	SS	MM	DD	D
I know	why	I'm so	sad, be-	cause my	name is	Billy	Sad.

When the game is played, one child sits in the middle and shows a very, very sad face. Another child is chosen to try to make the "sad child" laugh. The game can be really confusing socially because facial expressions are the point of the game (along with s-m-d). A social story book or pictures that include the steps of the game can help a student with autism become familiar with, and remember, the game. This can then, perhaps, be used as an example when the topic of facial expressions is discussed during music.

As a music teacher of a student with autism, it is important not to assume that a student understands the emotional intent or the emotional consequence of an event. Emotions are difficult for students with autism to decode. For example, from time to time you may be disappointed with a music class or an ensemble. You may need to have a heart-to-heart talk with the class because something did not meet your expectations musically or with the behavior of the group. If this occurs, it may be a lot for a student with autism to comprehend. She may not be able to process all that happened with such a discussion. She also may be more concerned with understanding your frustration than with the event that caused you to be frustrated in the first place.

It is important to work through the discussion and decode the emotions you were feeling with this student after the class discussion. Talk about how you felt and why you felt that way and how she may be able anticipate your frustration in the future. Also, it may be helpful to provide a signal for this student if her level of frustration rises again to prepare her and to allow her an opportunity to change her behavior.

Musically, it is important to be careful with abstract or emotional instructions. For example, in a band rehearsal of the chorale *Come Sweet Death* (Bach), a director may ask students to play a passage as if they were deeply saddened and it was the darkest day of their lives. This may require a band director to take time individually with a student and explain "darkest day of their lives" and what kinds of things might happen on a day like this, and work through their own emotional vocabulary. A student with high-functioning autism may have difficulty relating these emotions to technique on an instrument. Specific points of the discussion may include how to get a darker sound and how this relates to a Bach chorale. If explained in detail, the student may have a better chance to experience emotional performances with peers.

Imitation

There are three ways students with autism struggle in the area of imitation. First, students with autism have a difficult time transferring or imitating fine motor movements (similar to those examined in vignette 6.1).

Many students with autism not only lack fine motor skills, they also lack the motor planning to be able to imitate these movements. Carter and colleagues explain that "studies have consistently revealed that younger children with autism consistently have problems in the imitation of simple body movements and those that involve objects" (p. 320).

In music, it is important to keep in mind that most musical fine motor skills can be broken down to smaller, more manageable tasks. Take the opening vignette as an example. Maybe a goal on day one for Doug is to put his thumb in the correct position on the frog of the bow. When he has mastered this task, then move to the other fingers, and so on. The music teacher may also take video demonstrating exactly what was expected during practice time at home. Doug may then take the video home and practice (and so his parents can understand how to help him). By modifying expectations and accommodating the individual learning needs of students with autism, the music teacher can help the student be truly successful in a music classroom or ensemble. Some of the initial steps involved in developing imitation can allow the process of accommodating and modifying to begin and continue in a meaningful way.

The second area of imitation that causes students with autism to struggle is eliciting imitation. For example, a student with autism is less likely to say "look at me do this" than a typical peer. There are a variety of reasons for this, including, but not limited to, self-confidence, self-spontaneity, developmental delays, and interest. It is important for the music teacher to encourage these skills by noting when Doug is performing a skill correctly. This can be as easy as saying, "Look how Doug is holding the bow. Very nice Doug!" Meaningful and honest positive feedback can reinforce behaviors and create a feeling of community among all students in the class or ensemble.

The third area of struggle is spontaneity of imitation. Students with autism are less likely to spontaneously imitate another person. They may do so when asked; however, they may not have interest in imitating independently. Again, if someone like Doug *does* spontaneously imitate something musical (when he otherwise would not), it is important for a music teacher to enthusiastically highlight the imitation and encourage him to continue.

Peer Relationships and Social Interaction

Deficiencies in social skills often culminate in a lack of ability to establish and maintain peer relationships. Carter and colleagues explain that individuals with autism have "limited interest in social interaction and reduced initiation of social contact" (p. 323). We have also noticed in substantial work with children on the spectrum that self-efficacy may be to blame. Students with autism begin to understand their place in the social sphere of influence among their peers. Many have attempted to initiate and maintain play with peers; however, because of their lack of social skills, students with autism will eventually cease these initiations because of the mounting failures and lack of experience. This causes the student to retreat further into his own world. Another issue is that some students with autism have interests that do not match those of their peers. They may still be interested in things their peers have already moved away from such as children's books and videos. These asynchronous social interests can also further divide a student with autism from his chronological peers.

The literature shows that this dichotomy leads some students with autism to initiate contact with adults instead of with other children their age (Hauck, Fein, Waterhouse, & Feinstein, 1995). Researchers speculate this is because adults usually have greater tolerance for unusual behaviors. In almost every school situation, there are students who seek out adults when given an opportunity to choose a group on a field trip or in a relaxed atmosphere, rather than other students. The more global concern for persons with autism is the inability to maintain relationships with others. Yes, persons with autism can learn to initiate contact, have "one shot" activities with others, and reciprocate contact from another person. However, they often have few long-lasting relationships (Carter et al., 2005). Especially as they get older, their lack of social life can cause them to become more isolated.

Peer Relationships and Social Interaction in the Music Classroom

The abovementioned areas of difficulty experienced by students with autism become manifest when they interact with peers or their teachers. There are a few strategies that can assist a student when interacting with peers as well as educators. First, model appropriate exchanges between the music educator and the student with autism. For example, when saying hello to a student, insist on eye contact and an appropriate response. Also, notice the social interactions between the student and his peers, and be aware of any that are inappropriate. If the student's responses seem odd or inappropriate, redirect the student by modeling the appropriate response. There are many social songs that can be used for examples. They include

> *"The Wheels on the Bus"*
> *"Herman the Worm"*
> *"Old Mr. Rabbit"*
> *"Bounce High, Bounce Low"*
> *"How Do I Feel Today?"*

These exchanges can transfer to everyday music classroom exchanges such as taking turns on instruments, performing partner songs, and other musical exchanges between the student and the social structure around him. It is important to not only coach the student with autism but also to have his peers understand the classroom expectations as well (Laushey & Heflin, 2000). Sometimes peers can be the best teachers of appropriate social skills and can allow the best opportunities for these skills to improve (Rogers, 2000).

As the students get older and sometimes become higher functioning socially, it is important for music teachers to offer them opportunities to reconnect with their peers. Often, because students with autism start with a deficit of skills in their ability to connect socially, they never get the chance to try again to develop and maintain appropriate peer relationships. Creating this opportunity can be as simple as pairing a very social student with a student with autism in a group activity or as involved as the partner choir idea that we mention later in this chapter. The central idea is providing the opportunity.

REVERSE INCLUSION

In many public schools, there is a growing trend in self-contained classrooms for students on the autism spectrum. The authors have seen successful *reverse inclusion* models where members of a regular education class join this self-contained class for music. This is done for a variety of reasons, including assisting with social skills, awareness, and teaching compassion to students who do not have autism. Typical peers can be coached to "buddy up" with a student at whatever comfort level they have.

This technique also can be used with performing ensembles. Many ensembles, such as partner choirs, are very popular in some public schools for just this reason. The potential value of this opportunity to foster social relationships as well as to provide a musical outlet for older students with autism cannot be overstated.

A high-school choral director implemented reverse inclusion in a practical and meaningful way. She added a class to her schedule as an adaptive music elective for students with autism. Her new choir consisted of approximately 12 students. They rehearsed together to learn two songs for a concert performance. Other choral students who were neurotypical volunteered to come to class often to practice with the students and take turns singing with them in preparation for the performance. On the day of the performance, the students with autism were each guided by a neurotypical student onto the stage. They sang the songs with their choir friends and received tumultuous applause when they completed their performance and as they left the stage. The rest of the choral performances that evening were sung by students in the traditional choirs offered at the high school. The special program grew the next year, and the choral director began accepting volunteers on an application and audition basis only because so many students wanted to partner with the students who had autism in the adaptive choral class.

CONCLUSION

The specific strategies utilized in the socialization of students with autism can be unique. Social dysfunction is a key attribute of autism. Therefore, bringing a student with autism into the mainstream of social life in a classroom is crucial to his overall development. The more we can expand a student's joint attention, eye gaze, affective development, and peer relationships, the more developed his social capacity within a musical structure will become.

Many of these global issues are addressed in other resources as well as in this chapter. Figure 6.3 provides a list of other articles and chapters that also examine models for providing the best social-learning environment for students with autism.

Humans are inherently social. It is, therefore, critical that individuals with autism struggle to overcome these social deficits throughout their lives. It is also critical that students and adults who do not have autism understand that the social connections made with those who have autism are not completely the responsibility of the person who has the deficit. This responsibility lies with every individual as they seek to create social connections with those around them. Through increasing socialization among all students, including those with autism, music educators are beginning to model the importance of these human connections.

Hammel, A. M., & Hourigan R. M. (2011). Teaching Music to Students with Special Needs: A Label-free Approach. New York: Oxford University Press (**Chapter 5**)
Hourigan, R. M. (2009). The invisible student: Understanding social identity construction within performing ensembles. *Music Educators Journal,* 95(4), 34–38.

Figure 6.3
Other Resources on Socialization

REFERENCES

Bandura, A. (1997). *Self-efficacy: exercise of control*. New York: W.H. Freeman.

Carter, A. S., Davis, N. O., Klin, A., & Volkmar (2005). Social development in autism. In F. R. Volkmar, R. Paul, A. Klin, & D. Cohen (eds.), *Handbook of autism and pervasive developmental disorders* (pp. 312–334). Hokoken, NJ: John Wiley & Sons.

Hammel, A. M., & Hourigan R. M. (2011). *Teaching music to students with special needs: A label-free approach*. New York: Oxford University Press.

Hauck, M., Fein, D., Waterhouse, L., & Feinstein, C. (1995). Social initiations by autistic children to adults and other children. *Journal of Autism and Developmental Disorders, 25*(6), 579–595.

Hourigan, R. M. (2009). The invisible student: Understanding social identity construction within performing ensembles. *Music Educators Journal, 95*(4), 34–38.

Kanner, L. (1943). Autistic disturbances of affective contract. *Nervious Child, 2*, 227–250.

Laushey, K. M., & Heflin, J. L. (2000). Enhancing social skills of kindergarten children with autism through the training of multiple peers as tutors. *Journal of Autism and Developmental Disorders, 30*(3), 183–193.

Rogers, S. J. (2000). Interventions that facilitate socialization in children with autism. *Journal of Autism and Developmental Disorders, 30*(5), 399–409.

Theimann, K. S., & Goldstein, H. (2001). Social stories, written text cues, and video feedback: Effects on social communication of children with autism. *Journal of Applied Behavior Analysis, 34*, 425–446.

DISCUSSION QUESTIONS

1. Revisit the discussion questions in vignette 6.1. Having read this chapter, how would you answer these questions differently?
2. How could you expand joint attention and eye contact in your music classroom?
3. What are some modeling strategies you have seen work with students on the autism spectrum?
4. How can you encourage positive social interaction and lasting peer relationships in *your* music classroom?
5. How do you feel reverse inclusion would work with your students?

CHAPTER 7

Autism, Sensory Dysfunction, and Music Education

CHAPTER OVERVIEW

Many people with autism struggle with sensory integration challenges. This may have a large impact on their ability to learn music. This chapter addresses the following topics:

- Understanding sensory challenges
- Tactile strategies for the music classroom
- Visual strategies for the music classroom
- Vestibular and proprioceptive strategies in the music classroom
- Auditory strategies in the music classroom
- Sensory motor and motor planning
- How to address self-stimulating sensory behavior in the music classroom

---

One of the most challenging attributes of students with autism is that they sometimes demonstrate a dysfunction in sensory integration (DSI). Researchers who study autism have agreed that DSI is present "when the brain inefficiently processes sensory messages coming from a person's own body and his or her environment" (Kranowitz, 2006). In a classroom, this can appear to be a hypersensitivity (oversensitivity) or hyposensitivity (undersensitivity) to sensory information. Some students find taste, smell, touch, sound, and visual information to be insufficient, overwhelming, or both.

Studies have shown that 42%–80% of children with autism demonstrate unusual sensory responses (Kientz & Dunn, 1997). Researchers study sensory integration in the areas of tactile, visual, auditory, vestibular (balance and movement), proprioceptive (body position), olfactory (smell),

---

Vignette 7.1
ASHLEY

Today in music class, one of the song choices is "London Bridges." The students stand up from their chairs and make a line behind Sarah and Jeff, who form the bridge for the students to walk under. Ashley begins to be uncomfortable. As the children brush by her, she says, "Ouch!" Mr. Roberts goes over to hold her hand, and she pulls away and moves to the other side of the room. The more Mr. Roberts attempts to get Ashley to participate, the more resistant she becomes to interacting with her peers.

Discussion:
- What is making Ashley uncomfortable?
- How could Mr. Roberts engage Ashley?
- Whom should Mr. Roberts consult about today's class?

---

gustatory (taste), and sensory motor systems. We focus on all of the above (except the olfactory and gustatory integrations) as they apply directly to the music classroom.

People typically receive sensory information (e.g., touch, light, sounds, smells) and instantly make decisions based on this sensory neurological information. Our central nervous system processes stimuli and tells our body how to react. Children with DSI have difficulty differentiating between and among various stimuli (Kranowitz, 2006). They also sometimes respond inappropriately to sensory information or fail to respond at all to prompts given by others or their environment. As a result, a person with DSI cannot use the information gathered from stimuli to make adaptive responses (p. 6). To a typical person, these processes are automatic and can go unnoticed. For a child with sensory challenges, however, making adaptive responses to sensory stimuli is a constant struggle.

For example, when a neurotypical person comes upon a staircase as he walks down the street, he does not need to examine or contemplate how he may navigate the staircase; he just grabs the railing and starts down the stairs. A student with autism, who may also have motor-planning challenges, will approach a staircase and have a completely different experience. He may have trouble with several aspects of stair navigation. For example, he may need to concentrate on the gross motor movements, on moving one foot at a time down each step not knowing or remembering the distance between steps. He may have trouble feeling his feet touch the stairs or not know whether he should start the next step with the opposite foot. The action of walking down stairs requires that the visual, tactile, vestibular, and proprioceptive systems all work together. Receiving this sensory information, processing it, and then planning the next step are all under the umbrella of sensory integration.

This chapter examines challenges with sensory integration and music education. It explores each area of sensory integration (i.e., tactile, vestibular, proprioceptive, visual, auditory, and sensory motor) and provides lesson examples that enhance music classroom experiences for students with autism. This chapter is also an extension of the Hammel and Hourigan philosophy of using a label-free approach when teaching students with special needs. Many students with disabilities (not just those with autism) struggle with these areas of development. Instead of connecting a label to physical and sensory development, it is important to understand that sensory integration is part of a child's physical/sensory development. Understanding these areas of concern allows a music teacher to focus on a student's development and areas of relative strength and weakness rather than being consumed or confused with generalizations, etiologies, and labels.

TACTILE CHALLENGES IN THE MUSIC CLASSROOM

Many students with autism have tactile sensory sensitivity (Baranek, Parham, & Bodfish, 2005). Some students with autism do not want to be touched. When it happens, the student may shrivel into a ball to avoid unwanted sensory input. Conversely, some students attend music class wearing a weighted vest or regularly ask paraprofessionals for "a squeeze." Furthermore, some students like to be "brushed" or need other forms of sensory input to feel ready to learn and work with others. These are signs of tactile dysfunction.

Typically, tactile sensitivities manifest themselves in two ways. Some students may be hyposensitive or hypersensitive to touch. These students may appear similar to those described in the previous paragraph. Other students may have poor tactile discrimination (difficulty understanding how things feel). These students may have difficulty holding mallets or pencils. They may seem out of touch with their appendages and fingers. Both sensitivity level (hyper/hypo) and tactile discrimination are subsets of tactile dysfunction (Baranek, Parham, & Bodfish, 2005).

As we stated earlier, the occupational therapist in a district is the first person to consult if these issues arise in the music classroom. She will be able to provide some recommendations for a student who exhibits needs, as noted in vignette 7.1. For students who are hypersensitive or hyposensitive to textures or things they touch in your room, it is helpful to consider the following: (a) change textures (e.g., add felt to a mallet handle); (b) use time on and off musical equipment (e.g., today you will play the drum for two minutes; tomorrow, three minutes); (c) begin any music activity that involves touch by partnering with the music teacher (then try partnering with a student); and (d) connect desensitization activities with those occurring in other situations.

For students who are hyposensitive to tactile input, consider approaching the occupational therapist to become more educated about giving sensory input to the student (e.g., "head squeezes"; brushing; joint compression). This may allow music classes and rehearsals to continue without interrupting the flow and pacing. Many teachers are able to continue teaching while performing these tasks. Also, consider including the paraprofessional in these activities if one is currently part of the classroom environment.

VESTIBULAR AND PROPRIOCEPTIVE CHALLENGES IN THE MUSIC CLASSROOM

Music and movement coexist. Whether in a general music classroom or an orchestra, one truly doesn't exist without the other. Students with autism can have difficulty with vestibular movement. Kranowitz (2006) explains that "the vestibular system tells us where our heads and bodies are in relationship to the surface of the earth" (p. 60). Basic motor movements that involve these systems may be uncomfortable for students with autism. In music class, they may avoid basic movements such a hand signs, dance movements, finger games, or marching. In addition, students with autism may also have challenges with their proprioceptive sense. Kranowitz describes this sense as "sensory information telling us about the position, force, direction, and movement of our own body parts" (p. 88). Students who struggle in this area may be uncoordinated and have trouble with simple tasks, such as jumping or putting on shoes. In addition, to feel their body in space, they may pull or stretch their clothing.

Vignette 7.2

Karik is one of Ms. Hutti's favorite students. However, every time she schedules a song that requires movement, Karik withdraws to the point of having a meltdown in class. When she attempts to encourage him to dance with other students, he says "no!" emphatically and usually causes a disruption.

Discussion:
- What are the sensory issues with Karik?
- How would you attempt to involve Karik with the rest of the class?

Modes of vestibular dysfunction fall under the same categories as tactile dysfunction and are all derivatives of sensory dysfunction. A student can be either oversensitive, underresponsive, or have poor discrimination when processing balance and movement stimuli. Figure 7.1 lists these areas as well as issues to consider when adapting lessons with movement in mind.

Many active music classrooms include music and folk dancing. These activities can be successfully implemented in classes that include students who have difficulty with vestibular hypo- and hypersensitivities. One accommodation is to have the student who is hypersensitive wear gloves (if the gloves do not cause further sensory confusion) during games and dances that involve touching others or holding hands. Some teachers have had great success using air clapping instead of actual hand-to-hand contact. Students learn quickly that the games and dances go very well when they adjust their expectations based on the partner in front of them. Once a student who is learning to be more or less sensitive to touch knows that his needs will be met, a great deal of his anxiety dissipates.

Students who are hyposensitive to touch may squeeze hands or clap hands with great strength. This is because they are unable to feel the other hand or arm unless they engage the other student with more force than the other student is accustomed to receiving. This can cause pain and misunderstanding between students. This student may also need to wear gloves or hold either end of a rhythm stick, mallet, or rope during the activity. Again, once these procedures are in place, the activities can be seamless and inclusive.

Hypersensitive (to movement and balance): Student may appear intolerant and may avoid music activities such as dance and other movement activities.

Accommodations to consider: Ease the student in. For example, if using a movement component, break the movement down into smaller segments. Add segments as the student becomes comfortable. Also use time in and time out of the activity.

Hyporesponsive (to movement and balance): Student may crave spinning, rocking, or jumping, and may not ever get dizzy.

Accommodations to consider: Use this to your advantage. There are plenty of spinning, rocking, and fast movement songs and exercises available. Important note: student may need this type of movement incorporated with a sensory break.

Poor Discrimination (to movement or balance): Student may lose his balance easily when climbing stairs, jumping, or even standing.

Accommodations to consider: This can be a safety issue. Consult with the special education team before attempting to adapt a lesson. Make sure you have a full understanding of the limitations a student may have.

Figure 7.1
Vestibular Dysfunction Areas and Accommodations for the Music Classroom

Vignette 7.3
JEFF

Jeff is one of Mr. Wollet's favorite students. However, in orchestra, Jeff always squints. Mr. Wollet has also noticed that Jeff gets lost very easily when the music moves quickly. Jeff is an excellent musician and one of the top viola players in the ensemble. However, at the last concert, he missed entrances and did not do well on his solo. The stage lights seemed to really bother him.

Discussion:
- What are the challenges Jeff faces that are connected to sensory dysfunction?
- What accommodations can Mr. Wollet use in the classroom?
- What accommodations can Mr. Wollet use at a performance?

VISUAL DYSFUNCTION

Visual dysfunction is sometimes paired with loss of vision. For students with autism (who are otherwise sighted), there are often other challenges associated with visual dysfunction. Students may be sensitive to lights (halogen) or have difficulty shifting focus. Some students have difficulty crossing the midline of the body or touching an exact spot on a piece of paper. As we mentioned in chapter 2, all these challenges should be listed in the student's IEP.

An occupational therapist (see chapter 2) is the first person to speak with when discovering or learning about visual sensory needs. Occupational therapists are highly trained individuals who have great ideas regarding the accommodation of students who have visual sensory needs. Figure 7.2 presents some general ideas for accommodations or adaptations that can be made for students who are challenged in this area.

Adaptations are similar to those described in figure 7.1. All the areas discussed in this chapter are within the overall category of sensory dysfunction. However, some challenges may decrease over time. With practice, many students can learn to compensate for these sensory issues.

In a secondary choral setting, a student who struggles in the area of visual orientation may be unable to focus on the black print that is prevalent in most choral octavos. Placing a transparency over the page may soften the stark difference between the white paper and the black print and help the student see the words and notes on the page. Another successful strategy is to highlight the choral part the student will be singing. This allows him to focus his vision only on the important elements he is singing, without the constant filtering of ancillary information that is not necessary for his

Light Sensitivity: Turn off standard school lights and use lamps. Christmas tree lights and other ancillary lighting are also recommended. If this is impossible, allow the student to wear sunglasses.

Tracking or Changing Areas of Focus: Consider evaluating movement (how fast/slow and how much movement exists) in a given class period. Videotape a lesson or rehearsal. Slow down and allow more transition time. Also, have a "buddy" or paraprofessional track music with their finger for the student. Enlarge music. Highlight sections and eliminate unnecessary information (e.g., pictures or copyright information)

Spatial Relationships: When describing up, down, right, left, etc., model the appropriate action. Move the student to a marimba (instead of bells) to provide a larger target for mallets.

Figure 7.2
Sensory Visual Accommodations for Students in the Music Classroom

participation. Once the student has learned the piece, the highlighted lines can be erased using an erasable highlighter so that the octavo may be used again with a student who does not need this accommodation.

AUDITORY SENSITIVITY AND DYSFUNCTION

Auditory sensitivity can be problematic for students with autism in music classrooms. Music is often loud, and there are sounds that are uncommon to the student. Students in music classrooms sometimes have difficulty receiving and interpreting the finer details of conversations or directions. For example, a teacher may give directions to write two measures of 4/4 time that contain quarter and paired eighth notes on a page of staff paper. The student with autism may hand in the page with just a quarter note or a quarter note and an eighth note without understanding the specifics of the assignment. A successful strategy when working with students who have autism is to include visual directions for all students whenever aural directions are used. These directions may be written or pictorial depending on the needs of the student.

Auditory dysfunction is often paired with language development issues. This is one reason students with autism progress slowly in the area of receptive language (Eikeseth & Hayward, 2009). Verbal comprehension and the discrimination of sounds are also central to a student's ability to learn music. Therefore, it is imperative for music teachers to consult the special education team, review the IEP, and determine if a student has auditory sensitivities that may affect learning.

Adaptations and accommodations may include using headphones to block loud sounds, using simplified language, accompanying spoken instructions with written or pictorial information, and accompanying language with modeling. A successful strategy is to create a classroom culture that encourages soft voices, purposeful sound, and sensitivity to the aural needs of all students. When their aural sensorial needs are accommodated, students with autism are often more successful in the music classroom.

SENSORY MOTOR/MOTOR PLANNING/DYSPRAXIA

Motor planning is another area of dysfunction that has a direct effect on a student's ability to learn in the music classroom. Whether it is the movement involved in a singing game or activity, or putting the hands in the correct place on a drum, the steps in between can be difficult for a student with autism. This leads to another challenge for many persons with autism. Dyspraxia (or dysfunction in praxis) is the "difficulty conceiving of, planning, organizing, and carrying out a sequence of unfamiliar actions" (Kranowitz, 2006). Many people with autism (and other disabilities) struggle with dyspraxia since they lack the motor skills to coordinate movement in concert with the rest of their bodies.

Research on motor skills is divided into two broad categories. The first is "executive planning," which is "a sequence of choices or moves that must be arranged in order to achieve the desired in state (a goal)" (Swieten, Williams, Plumb, Van Bergen, Wilson, & Kent, 2010, 493). "Motor planning" involves the actions in between the steps needed to achieve a goal. For example, if a child desires to climb to the top of the stairs, she needs to plan to climb to each step (executive planning). In addition, she will need to bend her knees, raise her foot, and place her foot on the next stair, and then continue the pattern (motor planning). This is often difficult for persons with autism.

Motor planning may also be difficult for a student who is attempting to learn music. However, for a music teacher, accommodations may be more obvious than for some other areas mentioned in this chapter or even in this book. Effective instruction in the area of motor planning involves dividing the steps of a task into small units. Movement activities, instruments, and song motions all have increments that can be advantageous. By creating task analyses of motor planning activities, students can learn to "chunk" (break into small pieces) these skills for eventual success when performing the entire skill or activity.

Both the occupational therapist and the physical therapist assigned to the school or students are the first line of contact when designing accommodations, adaptations, and modifications for a student with motor planning issues. By including other professionals, you are able to learn from their years of experience and transfer their suggestions directly to your

1.	Put the case on lap.
2.	Look for green sticker that indicates the top of the case to be sure it is ready to be opened.
3.	Open the latches of the case.
4.	Take the reed from the reed case and put it in your mouth.
5.	Remove the lower joint from the case with your left hand. This joint is marked with a piece of blue tape.
6.	Remove the bell from the case with the right hand.
7.	Attach the bell to the lower joint (see picture).
8.	Hold the lower joint and bell (after attachment) with your right hand.
9.	Remove upper joint from the case with the left hand.
10.	Put the three fingers of the left hand down on the upper joint (see picture).
11.	Attach the upper joint to the lower joint while three fingers are still down on the upper joint.
12.	Hold the upper joint, lower joint, and bell with the left hand.
13.	Remove the barrel from the case.
14.	Attach the barrel to the upper joint using the left hand.
15.	Remove the mouthpiece from the case.
16.	Attach the mouthpiece to the barrel using the left hand.
17.	Remove the ligature from the case.
18.	Place the ligature over the mouthpiece with the wider side first (see picture).
19.	Take reed out of mouth.
20.	Slide reed in between ligature and mouthpiece.
21.	Align the tip of the reed with the top of the mouthpiece (see picture).
22.	Tighten screws on the ligature.
23.	All ready to play!

Figure 7.3
A Task Analysis for Assembling a Clarinet

lesson plans. Because music educators are often less knowledgeable about the intricacies of motor issues, this collaboration can be very helpful.

An example of a motor planning activity that can be overwhelming to a student is the assembly of a clarinet. Students who are working to improve their motor planning abilities may have difficulty assembling this instrument; however, if the clarinet is the instrument chosen, accommodations can be made to assist in the motor planning portion. The information in figure 7.3 can be placed in a book or on a series of pages, with photos, to remind a student of the executive planning necessary when assembling the clarinet.

SELF-STIMULATING SENSORY BEHAVIORS

Some music educators have taught a student with autism who engages in a behavior such as flapping his hands or in other stereotypical behaviors that appear to have no function. These behaviors are common among persons with autism. Sometimes they provide a pleasing sensory feeling for the student. Therefore, students with autism will engage in stimming (continuing these behaviors repeatedly for self-stimulation).

These behaviors can be a challenge for a music teacher. They can detract from learning for the student with autism as well as for the other students in the classroom. It is important to determine, with the assistance of an occupational therapist, the intent of these behaviors and if there is anything you can do to decrease or eliminate them (if they need to be) and redirect the student to music learning. Sometimes, however, these behaviors are necessary to the student's learning or attending in the classroom or ensemble. In essence, the student must engage in these behaviors for learning to take place because of the calming effect they have on his sensory motor system. The occupational therapist is almost always able to help you decide if or how a behavior may be shaped. If the behavior is a must for the student with autism, the task becomes orienting other students to the need and desensitizing them until they no longer attend to the student when he engages in his self-stimulating behaviors. A music teacher *should not* interrupt or try to curb the behavior without a consultation with a special educator or service provider. This may result in a meltdown or a major disturbance in the classroom.

Because these behaviors may seem odd to other students, it may be appropriate (after consultation with the special education team) to discuss the need of the student with autism to move in his specific way, and to discuss how this student and other students in classroom can learn while this movement is occurring. This is especially important if the behavior could result in a safety concern with other students. Once students are aware of the procedures to follow in the event the student with autism engages in the self-stimulating behavior, the lesson may continue without interruption, other than to move away from the student or to redirect attention elsewhere. These conversations are most effective when they are a team effort and the result of discussions with the paraprofessionals, special education faculty, and service providers.

CAUTIONARY CONSIDERATIONS

- The basic adaptations and accommodations for students with special needs can also be effective for students with autism. Every child is different, and his or her needs can be met by using common methods and materials adaptations. See *Teaching Music to Students with Special Needs: A Label-Free Approach* (Hammel & Hourigan, 2011).
- Do not forget the importance of the team approach when adapting instruction to suit the sensorial needs of students with autism. Therapists and service providers can be invaluable.

SENSORY BREAKS (CONCLUSION)

The overarching message for music teachers who encounter the challenges described in this chapter is to understand that a student with autism experiences considerable stress when faced with these issues. If a student is sensitive to sound, he is going to be concerned about the classroom where he last experienced uncontrolled or loud noises. If he is in a room with loud noises for a long period of time, he may need time away from the environment or other physical accommodations when participating in that environment.

The term "sensory break" is used in these circumstances. Teachers often discuss the content and patterns of these sensory breaks. These patterns are then used to give a student time away to collect himself or reach a state of equilibrium before returning to the classroom or activity. If a student knows he will be allowed to take a break, he may be less anxious about completing a task or participating in a music activity.

Often, there are "sensory rooms" in school buildings that may have soothing items available for students. These can be quiet places for them to restore their sensory balance. Students may use this room as a retreat from the sensory overload they experience during the day. Consult with the special education team about the best use of sensory breaks within your lesson sequence. Understanding and adapting to his sensory needs may make a tremendous difference in the overall success the student with autism experiences in music.

Teaching compassion and acceptance in a music classroom creates a culture that allows for differences and rejoices in new steps toward success. The act of inclusion can create a kinder and more conscious learning environment for all students. This environment, in turn, can lead to a culture that is focused on the individual's success as well as the group goals in classrooms and ensembles. It also exemplifies the basic tenets of inclusion.

REFERENCES

Baranek, G. T., Parham, D. L., Bodfish, J. W. (2005). Sensory and motor features in autism: Assessment and intervention. In F. R. Volkmar, R. Paul, A. Klin, & D. Cohen (eds.), *Handbook of autism and pervasive developmental disorders* (pp. 831–857). Hokoken, NJ: John Wiley & Sons.

Eikeseth, S. and Hayward, D. W. (2009). The discrimination of object names and object sounds in children with autism: A procedure for teaching verbal comprehension. *Journal of Applied Behavior Analysis, 42*(4), 807–812.

Kientz, M. A., & Dunn, W. (1997). A comparison of the performance of children with and without autism on the sensory profile. *American Journal of Occupational Therapy, 51,* 530–537.

Kranowitz, C. S. (2006). *The out-of-sync child has fun.* New York: Perigee.

Swieten, L. M., Williams, J. H., Plumb, M. S., Van Bergen, E. Wilson, A. D., Kent, S. W. (2010). A test of motor (not executive) planning in developmental coordination disorder and autism. *Journal of Experimental Psychology, 36*(2), 493–499.

DISCUSSION QUESTIONS

1. How will you know a student is having a sensory issue?
2. What accommodations can you create for a student who has vestibular or proprioceptive sensory needs in the music classroom?
3. What accommodations can you create for a student who has auditory or visual sensory needs in the music classroom?
4. What accommodations can you create for a student who has tactile sensory needs in the music classroom?
5. Do you have a place in your school where a student can take a sensory break? If so, describe the room.

CHAPTER 8

Advocacy for Students with Autism in Music Education

CHAPTER OVERVIEW

Music students with autism are frequently placed in music learning environments that are not conducive to their needs. Music educators must advocate for the best learning environment for their students. This chapter focuses on the following topics:

- Establishing relationships with parents, special educators, special education administrators, and classrooms teachers to advocate for the most appropriate learning environment
- Understanding the necessary components of the musical learning environment for students with autism
- Reaching out to community organizations for support

Many students who are challenged by autism have a unique relationship with music. Unfortunately, students on the autism spectrum are frequently denied an enriching music education that fosters a life-long relationship with the arts. Many are placed in classrooms with unfavorable learning conditions or situations that do not adequately support music teachers with training and staff support. As advocates for music education, we must not only advocate for inclusion of students with autism in music, but also for the appropriate placement and support of students with autism within those music education classes.

This chapter is designed to offer suggestions for music educators in the area of advocacy by offering strategies and suggestions for fostering relationships with parents, special educators, teachers, and community organizations, with the aim of supporting all music students. It outlines the research-informed learning conditions that must exist for a student with autism to learn, as well as the research-based competencies that must exist for successful school music instruction for students with autism. It is hoped that after reading this chapter, music teachers will understand the attributes of successful and proper access to the music education curriculum and strategies to enhance appropriate placement opportunities.

FOSTERING RELATIONSHIPS WITH ALL STAKEHOLDERS

To secure the best learning environment for a student with autism, a music teacher must develop relationships with other professional members of the faculty as well as parents. To do this, music teachers must first understand the perspectives of the various stakeholders who participate in the life of a student with autism. The members of the team all come to the table with various needs and interests as well as different day-to-day experiences. As professionals, it is appropriate to consider these differing perspectives when advocating for the best musical experience for specific students with autism.

Parents

To be truly effective in advocating for appropriate placement of students with autism in music classrooms and ensembles, the first contact the music teacher makes is often the parents. When interacting with parents, it is important to remember that they were initiated into a life of seeking appropriate treatments for their child without much prior training or experience. This initiation often involves sorting out confusing advice, making countless trips to various medical professionals and therapists, as well as managing the ever-changing challenges of raising their child with ASD. Ryan and Cole (2009) state:

> The role of advocate is familiar to many parents. Parents intercede on behalf of their children at school, at clubs, or in the street and this advocacy continues into adulthood. However, for parents of disabled children, evidence suggests that the advocacy role develops to a level of frequency and complexity, which other parents do not face. (p. 43)

Vignette 8.1 is the story of a parent and child with autism. The boy is only eight years of age. A considerable amount of advocacy may already have occurred in the life of a family before they reach the music classroom.

Vignette 8.1 demonstrates that parents may come into the school with a variety of perspectives and experiences with education professionals. Some of these experiences are positive and some are negative. They may or may not have had the best experience advocating for the most appropriate learning environment for their child. It is important to tread lightly when initiating contact with parents. Parents will respond best when they know teachers are looking for the most comfortable, best chance for their child to learn in the music classroom.

When interacting with parents, focus on the positive attributes their child brings to the class or ensemble. It is helpful to discuss the student in terms of strengths and areas of challenge, rather than to discuss labels and perceived deficits. If the parents bring up the subject of autism, the conversation may then pivot in that direction. By allowing the parents to control this aspect of the conversation, the music educator honors the personhood, rather than the label, of the student. Focus on the best music teaching and learning situation for their child. If their children can enjoy and succeed in music class, it will be a welcome relief for them. Many parents appreciate this approach and, after the relationship has been established, may become strong advocates for music education. This can be a rewarding experience for music educators who sincerely strive to be the best teachers possible for *all* their students.

Vignette 8.1
KIM AND BRIAN

I have always had a strong faith that the special education system is made up of dedicated individuals who share a parent's desire for an IEP that is well-written and well-executed. I also knew that even the best systems can have their weaknesses, making it all the more important that parents act as strong advocates when it comes to their children's education.

When we enrolled in the New Orleans school system, we did not come empty-handed. Our son was eight years old, had a well-planned IEP, and had already received educational services for five years. But there I was, being told that my son, who is blind, developmentally delayed, and has autism, would be placed in a second-grade classroom. Just as I was trying to fathom how he would manage in a second-grade classroom, she noticed he was eight years old, and told me he would have to be in the third grade based on his age. Thinking there was a misunderstanding, I said, "Well, in Indiana, he was in a moderate disabilities classroom." The special education teacher told me they did not have a special education classroom at this school. All children were mainstreamed. "But he will have an aide, to assist him?" I asked, beginning to get worried. "No," she told me. She said they did not have the staffing to provide him with an aide.

Brian was placed in a third-grade classroom (without an aide). I suggested I could accompany him on his first day of school—just to help people understand what his needs were and answer any questions they might have. Everyone thought that was a good idea. Brian was introduced to his third-grade teacher, and I wondered if that teacher knew what was in store for him. I am not saying this because I think my son is a "bad" kid or a "hard to like" kid, I am saying this because I immediately began to think about all of the responsibilities that were going to be placed on the shoulders of a regular education teacher who had no training in special education (let alone autism or vision impairment) and 20+ other students he would have to manage.

Brian needed assistance in so many ways. From an academic perspective, he would need Braille materials, audio books, and tactile devices when the other students were using visual aids. Beyond this, Brian's language was very limited. His ability to comprehend was tested at a 2- to 3-year-old level, and his ability to express himself tested even more delayed. How would he follow basic classroom instruction or engage with peers without any assistance? He also lacked many of the independence skills we take for granted in a typical third grader. He needed full assistance to eat his lunch or use the restroom. He would require help moving around the classroom or building. How would his teacher manage all of this and still teach 20+ other students who had needs of their own?

I sat next to Brian in his classroom and watched as one teacher passed around worksheets for everyone to complete. She placed one in front of Brian without even questioning how he was going to meaningfully participate in this exercise without assistance. Later, she gave all the children (including Brian) a blank sheet of paper and asked them to draw pictures of things that were red. When I expressed my concerns to my school administrator, her response to me was, "Well, we do things differently down here. You just need to give it a chance." Different, I can accept. Inclusion, I can even support when executed properly. What they were doing, I would call "dumping" (putting a student in an inclusive environment without needed supports).

After accompanying Brian to school for numerous days, I finally told my husband, "I want you to go to the special education administration building and sit there until *somebody* speaks to you!" (I could not go, as I was still in the third grade with my son.) Thus began a year-long struggle to get our son appropriately placed. Fortunately, someone came to see him right away. The person he spoke with was surprised to hear that I was attending school with Brian every day (even though Brian's administrative coordinator knew I was there every day) and immediately started contacting schools to see if we could move Brian. She even took Brad [Kim's husband] out to a school that very day so that he could see if it would be appropriate for Brian.

At the second school, we, along with Brian's teacher, fought to get Brian out of third grade. The administrators wanted to compromise by having Brian in the third grade part of the day, and in a resource room the other part of the day. We pushed to have him placed in first or second grade (which we thought was *still* too advanced for him). We even met with the administration and a representative from the Louisiana State Department of Education to again request a paraprofessional for Brian, and to demand he be taken out of the third grade. I took the grade-level expectancies— GLEs—for kindergarten, first grade, second grade, and third grade. (GLEs outline the skills a child should have acquired in order to complete a grade.) At that point in time, Brian did not meet even 20% of the GLEs for kindergarten, and out of about 200 GLEs for first grade, we could see that he was only competent in two. I asked everyone, "If he was a regular education student, and he only mastered 20% of kindergarten GLEs, would he be promoted to the third grade?" I was told that he was too big to be in kindergarten or first grade. I was also told that I "didn't really know how much he might be absorbing by being in the third-grade classroom."

I told that person that I found it offensive for her to suggest that I might not be picking up on academic developments in my own child, with whom I spend a great deal of time. Later I thought, "Yeah, but if a tree falls in the woods, and no one hears it, can we really call that learning?" (i.e., if knowledge is magically acquired, but not demonstrated, is it still labeled knowledge gained?) It was decided he would bump down to second grade for two months, and then back up to third. In reality, his teacher simply reduced the amount of time he spent in regular education and his teacher (who was supposed to be his Visual Impaired, or V.I., teacher) started attending regular ed. with him (so she was now acting as a para, or aide, and no longer teaching him Braille).

Over the course of that year, we called several case conferences, and requested due process. By that summer, we were co-complainants in a lawsuit against the Louisiana Dept. of Education. Not surprisingly, we searched for, found, and applied to a school that had a full special education program. There, he got a one-on-one para, he was moved to a special education classroom, and he was no longer required to spend time in academic regular education programs. He does interact with regular education students, but these interactions are designed more for his skill building and social-skills building, so he is not required to sit through a lecture on graphs or anything like that.

Finally, I am not writing this to demonize the entire education system. But again to point out that within every system there may be elements that are not working, and it is a parent's responsibility to make sure those areas are addressed. For when my energy to continue this endeavor to get appropriate services for my son began to flag, it was one of many highly skilled, dedicated, hardworking educators who told me, "Kim, as a parent, you are Brian's first teacher, and you will always be his best teacher. Believe that you know what is best for him, as you will be the one to witness the results years from now."

Discussion:

1. What would you do if you were Kim? Would you have done anything differently?
2. How has this vignette changed your attitude about parents of students with disabilities?

Special Educators

Special educators can be the best advocates for music and students with autism. In their own settings, they see the success students on the spectrum often have with music. Access to an appropriate music education within a proper placement can start with a special educator in an IEP meeting. She may have the leverage and a knowledge of the options available to create the best LRE choices for a student. She may also be able to articulate the reasons a student must be included in music and why it is beneficial to him. Therefore, spending time learning about the special educators who teach a student can be an effective advocacy tool for a music education program. Vignette 8.2 is an example of how a special educator can advocate for the best opportunities for a student with autism in band.

Vignette 8.2
MR. STANDISH

Working with students with special needs is both challenging and rewarding. For me, it is especially rewarding to work with students on the spectrum. My greatest joy comes from witnessing a student with autism accomplish a goal for the very first time. The smiles and joy expressed by these remarkable students are enough to warm any heart. The joy the students experience is the reason I strongly advocate for each individual, allowing him/her to pursue his/her talents and dreams. This is especially true when those talents and dreams lie within the framework of the fine arts.

I currently have a student that is absolutely gifted in music. My goal is not only to ensure that he has the opportunity to participate in band, but that he participates at a level equal to that of his talent. For this to be accomplished honest communication has to take place between the student, myself, the band instructor, and the parents.

The current issue is that the student plays by ear and does not read music. His band instructor wants him to read the music, which is a worthy goal, yet the student only looks at the music for a very short amount of time when playing. After learning of this concern, and talking with the parents, I met with the band instructor to brainstorm ways to help the student.

First, I had to define the goal in my non-musical mind. Do we want the student to play the music or do we want/need him to actually read the music. The band instructor told me that he enjoys the student and realizes that the student is incredibly gifted but, he feels that teaching to student to read music at this age will benefit the student significantly in the future. So we agreed that reading music is the goal. But, the student will continue to play in the band whether or not we can teach him to read music.

Next, our conversation led to how to accomplish our goal. Knowing that students with autism are usually very routine oriented, in my mind the music staff could be a very systematic visual guide once the student learned to read music. With this in mind, I suggested enlarging the music and presenting it to the student one stanza, or one line, at a time. Then slowly add more to the page and reduce the size, over time, until the student is used to reading music as it is usually printed.

Also, knowing the colors can be very symbolic, especially to students on the spectrum, I suggested color coding the notes by using a variety of highlighters. For example, an A could not be yellow, B green, C blue, etc. (Again, realize I have a very limited musical background.) Doing this could help the student associate the position of the notes on the staff with the color of the notes. Finally, I suggested using computer software and have the student play notes and watch them appear on the stanza. This would give him an instant visual cue to associate with each note that he plays. Essentially, he could "see" the music. Once he understands this concept it could be reversed. He would see the music (read it) and then produce the music as he plays.

The band instructor was pleased with my suggestions and indicated that they were each worth trying. In time, we will see if any of these steps help the student to accomplish the goal of reading music. In the meantime, continuous collaboration and support with the band instructor will allow this student to stay in band and for him to participate at the level equated with his gift.

Craig Standish
Muncie Public Schools
Muncie, Indiana

As we noted in chapter 2, when building a relationship with special educators, the first strategy is to acknowledge their expertise. This may include inviting teachers to the music classroom and asking their advice regarding effective strategies for working with students with autism. When advocating for the best musical fit for a student, we recommend that music teachers stress the positive life skills that a student also learns in the music program (social interaction, life-long enjoyment of music communication, etc.) and to highlight ways to assess and address challenges a student may have during participation in music instruction. Concerns (about behavior, engagement, etc.) may be resolved more easily if a positive relationship with special education colleagues has been established, and a team approach can be used to address issues regarding placement and participation. It is important for music teachers to have a collegial, professional relationship with the special education faculty and staff.

CAUTIONARY CONSIDERATIONS

- Do not unwittingly deny a student with autism the opportunity for aesthetic experiences by assuming the student will not understand. Many students, because of their challenges, cannot express the value of their own experiences. Often, children with autism are left out of arts experiences because of these reasons

Special Education Administrators

Special education administrators are often former or current special educators and possess many of the attributes we mentioned in the previous section. There is, however, an important distinction. These professionals are also on the administrative team and sometimes have access to and leverage with upper-level administrators and school board members, as well as the ability to change schedules and effect other accommodations that special education classroom teachers cannot accomplish alone. In some cases, special education administrators can also provide teachers with knowledge of policy that goes beyond the expertise of the special educator of record. Conversely, be mindful not to go over the head of a special educator. Whenever possible, talk with the special educator of record before going to the administrator. He may refer you to the special education administrators if there is an issue that is outside his realm of experience, or if he is not authorized to make certain decisions.

Classroom Teachers

The most important relationships to establish are with other teachers who teach the same student(s) with autism. Inclusion is meant to be a team effort; it is not effective as a solo effort. Sharing techniques, resources, and other items is crucial to success. It is also advised to remain as consistent as possible with expectations and communication strategies. Classroom teachers can also assist with any advocacy issues that arise. This is especially true if a positive and collegial relationship has been established and maintained.

When developing relationships with other teachers, it is essential to be seen as an advocate for a complete education. Music teachers must understand that in the current political climate, classroom teachers are compelled to make sure all students (including those with special needs) score well on state-sponsored standardized tests. They may not initially see the importance of the music curriculum in relationship to math, English, and science. In addition, many special educators teach oversized classes that include unfairly categorized classrooms and students. They may be under intense pressure.

Stress musical contributions to the general education curriculum during conversations with other teachers. For example, in a choral music classroom, comprehensive musicianship includes learning meaning and fluency in language. Ask for ways cross-curricular goals, ideas, and themes can be incorporated into the music classroom. This strengthens the relationship and provides students (with or without autism) with consistency within a reinforced curriculum.

CONDITIONS FOR MUSIC LEARNING FOR STUDENTS WITH AUTISM

Another area of advocacy is the appropriate placement and learning conditions of students with autism in music classrooms. Some students are placed in music classrooms without the proper support for learning. In addition, music teachers who teach students with autism often do not receive the appropriate information and support when teaching students with autism. This is not conducive for music learning for students with autism.

There is new research regarding learning conditions that foster music learning among students with autism and other disabilities and their experiences in music classrooms (Gerrity, Hourigan, and Horton, 2013; Blair 2009; Bell 2008; Burnard 2008; Haywood 2005; and Hammel 1999). Based on this research, the following section outlines the environmental conditions that best suit a student with autism in a music classroom. Music educators can use this research-informed information to advocate for the best learning environment for students with autism.

Learning Environment

Because of the sensory, communication, physical, social, and behavioral needs of students with autism, the learning environment must be constantly examined. Music teachers may need to adjust lights, consider class size, and consider seating (away from distractions). This may require a music educator to advocate for a different class placement (smaller, different time, different set of students) to achieve a Free and Public Education (FAPE) for a specific student.

Music educators may need to purchase items (e.g., lamps, headphones) that are not commonly listed in a music education budget. Purchasing these items may be facilitated through a request of the IEP or Case Study team. If a specific accommodation or adaptation is listed in a student's IEP or 504 Plan, it is a requirement to provide that specific item or service. Music educators may also investigate a collaborative partnership with a classroom teacher to request communication assistive devices such as iPads or other more costly devices that may necessary for the student to be successful across the curriculum. A suggested list of apps is available in chapter 10.

One-on-One Support

Many students with special needs require one-on-one assistants. Paraprofessionals can serve as a conduit between the music educator and a student with autism. Research has shown that paraprofessionals also need the support of a music educator. Paraprofessionals often have no formal music training, and may be unsure about when to assist and when to allow a student to attempt content on her own. It is to the music teacher's advantage to spend time with the paraprofessional to gain insight into the learning styles of the student with autism and to organize the music class or ensemble time to be as consistent as possible with the balance of the school day as experienced by the student.

Often, because of scheduling, paraprofessionals take breaks during music class. This break time may be indicated in the IEP or 504 Plan. It may be that the music class or ensemble time is the only time of day the paraprofessional can eat or use the restroom. If the music educator considers the presence of the paraprofessional, or other adult, necessary to appropriately accommodate a student with autism, it may be important to have the paraprofessional, or another special education teacher, observe a portion of class to understand the specific needs of a student that are unmet without appropriate staffing. Appropriately including a student with autism may include additional equipment to manipulate, increased distractions, and a larger number of students who are experiencing different class routines. This is the time a paraprofessional may be *most* needed in the classroom with a student on the spectrum.

Multiple Ways to Demonstrate Knowledge

As has been stressed throughout this book, students with autism need to have many tools at their disposal to demonstrate their skills and understandings in music. In research and practice, the authors have found that coupling two types of response often affords an increased level of opportunity for a child to demonstrate knowledge. Verbal instructions paired with the opportunity to point at an icon or ask a student to show rather than tell the answer is a vital teaching technique in the music classroom.

If multiple avenues of expression do not exist for a child with autism, then advocacy becomes essential. For example, if a student needs access to picture icons, assistive communication devices, or paraprofessional support, then music teachers must attempt to be present at the IEP meeting to advocate for such items. Special educators may not know that the music teacher is in need of assistance. If presence at an IEP meeting is not possible, it is permissible to send a written account of progress in the music classroom with suggestions for additional support (aids or services). This is especially effective when it is clear that the request for information, services, and assistance is to allow the music teacher to be the best teacher she can be to that particular student.

Teacher Qualities That Must Exist in Music Classrooms

Alice Hammel's 1999 study of teacher competencies delineated techniques music teachers must understand, develop, and use to be successful when teaching students with special needs. In advocating for students with autism, figure 8.1 is a list of competencies to obtain when working with students on the spectrum.

Acquainted with various handicapping conditions.

Knowledge of Individuals with Disabilities Education Act (IDEA).

Knowledge of music teacher's role on evaluation team.

Able to develop and use informal assessment procedures.

Able to monitor the learning process of all students.

Able to evaluate program effectiveness for special learners.

Able to modify, if necessary, the instructional program to accommodate special learners.

Knowledge of how to modify the physical environment of a classroom for special learners.

Able to encourage appropriate social interactions among all students.

Knowledge of effective classroom management techniques.

Knowledge of appropriate materials for diverse learning abilities and styles.

Able to adapt materials to provide for individual differences.

Figure 8.1
14 Music Teacher Competencies
Source: Hammel, 1999.

CAUTIONARY CONSIDERATIONS

- Do not consider the least restrictive environment for a student with autism to be exclusively inclusion or exclusively self-contained. Some students work best in a fluid environment that is designed to meet their specific needs.

Much of the material in figure 8.1 has been discussed extensively in either this book or our previous book (Hammel & Hourigan, 2011). However, many music educators who read this material will not be the sole music provider in a building or school district. Music educators often have opportunities to work with student teachers or other pre-service music educators as well as to have conversations with colleagues about the students with autism included in the music classroom. Whether self-reflecting on teaching practices or encouraging the practices of others (e.g., colleagues, pre-service teachers), developing skills and understanding when teaching students with special needs (including those with autism) is a crucial part of the process.

LOCAL COMMUNITY NOT-FOR-PROFIT ORGANIZATIONS

Some music educators seek assistance from a local not-for-profit support group or agency. Often, these groups have grant programs for technology, instruments, or programs. These opportunities may arise because the organizations support the work being done in the music classroom. As a result, they may see the benefits of music for students on the autism spectrum, and ultimately fund successful music programs. Many of these organizations are listed in chapter 10. The *Autism Society of America* and *Autism Speaks* have local chapters nationwide. Many of the local chapter affiliates have grant programs that may be applicable to needs for students with autism in the music classroom.

PUBLIC "INFORMANCES" INCLUDING STUDENTS WITH AUTISM

Public programs and performance are great opportunities to advocate for music education. However, many students with autism struggle with these

CAUTIONARY CONSIDERATIONS

- Special education funding may be available for the music classroom if the need for the items is listed in the IEP. In addition, do not discount the possibilities for support that can come from the local community and special needs advocacy groups.
- Do not assume that students with autism and their families will not enjoy the opportunity to showcase their accomplishments in music even if they are not perfect in a traditional sense. Just getting one or two notes or a sequence of movements can be a powerful experience for a parent to witness. As a result, they may become your biggest advocate.
- Remember, do not neglect to develop the supportive and compassionate possibilities of pairing neurotypical students with students who have autism and other special needs.

types of events. If an included student, or self-contained class, can succeed as part of the schoolwide winter program with the assistance of paraprofessionals, then seize the moment to include the student in the program. Conversely, if the class needs a different setting or opportunity, brainstorm with the other special education team members to find an appropriate public venue.

This may be an *informance*. Set up a small performance area in a classroom and have the parents of the students who may not be able to participate in an all-school or large event join the class for one day. The parents may sit audience style or side-by-side with the students and participate in class activities. Make sure to invite administrators to the informance. This type of occasion, especially in a self-contained setting, can be very meaningful to parents, administrators, and other special educators. It is an opportunity for the stakeholders to join in the success their students with autism are having in the area of music. It can also be a powerful advocacy tool. The participants see the music learning process and how it connects with success in other areas. They will also see the passion and dedication a music educator has to *all* her students.

STUDENT SUPPORT AND AWARENESS GROUPS

The best way to raise awareness among students is to get them involved in supporting students with disabilities. Students can be great advocates and, as they get older, may become community members in leadership positions where they can support students with autism. For example, the Best Buddies organization (http://www.bestbuddies.org) pairs a junior high, high-school, or college student with an individual with developmental disabilities (including autism). These "buddies" go into the community and do the things that typical friends do, such as go to a movie or out to dinner. There are chapters in all 50 states and in 50 countries around the world.

From an advocacy perspective, other students can provide meaningful input into the social structure of the daily life of a person with autism. Most important, if students see their peers interacting and socializing with someone who has autism, they may be more inclusive in their own attitudes about persons with autism. The more students get to know other students on the autism spectrum, the less likely they will be to make uninformed judgments about them. Best Buddies is an excellent example of this sort of advocacy for those with autism.

CONCLUSION

Many strategies discussed above provide vehicles for conversations with all team members in the life of a student with autism. Whether starting the conversation with a special educator or advocating for a change in an IEP, music teachers should base their advocacy efforts on creating the most appropriate learning environment for students in the music classroom. However, it is also necessary to understand the perspective of other professionals in the district or region, as well as those of the parents of a student with autism. Teachers may have test scores to achieve. Parents may be tired because every day seems like another day of fighting for their child's rights. Therefore, it is critical for music educators to understand the paradigms of all involved before initiating a concern.

Music educators often see successes during a time of many challenges. As discussed throughout this text, those successful moments may be an imperative piece of a student's school life. Do not be afraid to stress the significance of these successes. When students become adults, music may be their connection to society. Because of a successful music educator, they may be able to participate in a church choir or community band. At the very least, they may be a life-long lover of music and enjoy recordings, concerts, and live performances on television. All these musical opportunities will enhance the quality of life for persons with autism.

REFERENCES

Bell, A. P. (2008). The heart of the matter: Composing music with an adolescent with special needs. *International Journal of Education and the Arts, 9*(9). Retrieved 10/19/2011, http://www.ijea.org/v9n9.

Blair, D. V. (2009). Fostering wakefulness: Narrative as a curricular tool in teacher education. *International Journal of Education and the Arts, 10*(19). Retreived 10/28/2011, http://www.ijea.org/v10n19.

Burnard, P. (2008). Inclusive pedagogies in music education: A comparative study of music teachers' perspectives from four countries. *International Journal of Music Education, 26*(2), 109–126.

Hammel, A. (1999). A study of teacher competencies necessary when including special learners in elementary music classrooms: The development of a unit of study for use with undergraduate music education students. Unpublished doctoral dissertation, Shenandoah University.

Hammel, A., & Hourigan R. M. (2011). *Teaching Music to Students with Special Needs: A Label-free Approach.* New York: Oxford University Press.

Haywood, J. S. (2005). Including individuals with special needs in choirs: Implications for creating inclusive environments. Unpublished doctoral dissertation, University of Toronto.

Hourigan, R. M. , Gerrity, K. W., & Horton, P. (In press). Perceptions of participants regarding the conditions that facilitate music learning among students with special needs: A Mixed Methods Inquiry. *Journal of Research in Music Education.*

Ryan, S., & Cole, K. R. (2009). From advocate to activist? Mapping the experiences of mothers of children on the autism spectrum. *Journal of Applied Research in Intellectual Disabilities, 22*, 43–53.

DISCUSSION QUESTIONS

1. Do you know a student with autism who has had trouble in his/her music placement? What would you do differently?
2. Do you know a parent of a child with autism? Have they spoken about their advocacy efforts?
3. Have you met the special education administrator in your district? Have you spoken about a child with special needs? How did the conversation develop?
4. Do you know of a local agency or support group in your area for autism? Have they helped you personally or your school?
5. Have you had an "informance"? How was it organized? Did you find it to be successful?

CHAPTER 9

Classroom and Ensemble Snapshots of Teaching Music to Students with Autism

CHAPTER OVERVIEW

This chapter contains short case studies or vignettes that were provided by music teachers in the field who are actively teaching students with autism. It also provides examination and discussion of possible generalizations to all music classrooms. Contributions include:
- Classroom-based vignettes and discussion
- Performance-based vignettes and discussion
- Strategies and tips for the music classroom

A book examining teaching music to students with autism would not be complete without real-world examples of music teachers accommodating students with autism in music classrooms. In addition to the various classroom- and ensemble-setting vignettes that appear throughout the book, this chapter provides further examples from classroom- and performance-based music classrooms in a variety of settings. It is hoped that the discussion questions and commentary that follow each vignette will provide music teachers with the perspective they need to generalize similar situations within their own classrooms.

CLASSROOM-BASED EXAMPLES OF TEACHING MUSIC TO STUDENTS WITH AUTISM

Vignette 9.1 is an example of a student-centered music teacher concerned about including students with autism in a music classroom with other neurotypical students. As demonstrated in the vignette, an appropriate placement can have exponential benefits for the student. We discussed the topic of successful placement in chapter 6. To be implemented correctly, a well-constructed team relationship must be in place. Joshua's music teacher, special education teacher, and peers were working together for Joshua. Also, "buddies" were rotated so that every student in the class had an opportunity to work with him.

Having the student attend multiple or different music classes, as Joshua did, is not uncommon. Often, special educators discuss life skills that can be taught through music. Notice that Berta also, as a result of this placement,

---

Vignette 9.1

JOSHUA

When I began teaching music at my current elementary school, we had a self-contained autism support classroom with four male students. These students were scheduled to attend music class with a fourth-grade classroom of regular education students. As I got to know these boys, I believed that they would benefit from having their own self-contained music class in addition to their regular fourth-grade class, so I began to meet with them for an additional 30 minutes per week. I realized that one student in particular, Josh, though largely nonverbal, was achieving things in music that astounded his special education teacher: he learned to make sounds in his head register, answered questions by using a picture board, participated by making sounds when it was his turn to chain a phrase in the rhyme, played the beat on the rhythm instruments, and would work with a partner during a folk dance. He had several buddies who rotated working with him each class. He also had a one-on-one paraprofessional to help him integrate. Because of his great strides, Josh's special education teacher and I agreed that Josh would benefit from attending additional music classes when possible. Josh began to attend a third-grade music class in addition to his fourth-grade music class and the self-contained autistic-support music class. Because I had the opportunity to work with Josh so often to meet his needs, I became the classroom teacher who would attend his IEP meetings. This was truly one of the highlights of my teaching career.

Berta Yee Hickox
Halifax School District, Pennsylvania

became more involved in IEP meetings and was asked to represent Joshua. This allows Berta to be more involved with the decisions that are made within Joshua's curriculum. It also maintains her central place within the team that makes decisions for all students with special needs in the school. Active participation in school life can greatly enhance the standing of a music teacher within the eyes of her colleagues. A music educator who will accept, or even seek, additional responsibilities will gain much more experience and insight regarding all aspects of the school community.

Vignette 9.2

MR. SHOULDICE

In my third year of being an elementary music teacher, I look forward to my class of students with autism with the utmost enthusiasm. It is now undoubtedly the highlight of my week. However, this was not always the case. When I started this position three years ago in late August, before the halls and classrooms were brimming with students, I scheduled a meeting with my building's principal to discuss the "specials" schedule for the coming year. I was new to this building and had typical questions regarding the start and end times of classes, the number of sections, and what the music room was like. My principal handed me a copy of the specials schedule, and at first glance it appeared ordinary. Then I spotted the first 30-minute time-slot on Thursday morning labeled ASD. "What kind of class is this?" I asked. He replied, "Here at Brooks Elementary we service many of the district's students with autism."

I think that I was able to mask my initial apprehension from my principal, but I could definitely feel my heart pumping a little faster. I didn't have any previous experience with students with autism outside of one day spent learning about students with special needs in my undergraduate program. Autism sounded very scary, and I had serious doubts about my ability to teach such a class. Teaching students with autism was certainly uncharted territory for me. The principal suggested that I speak to the ASD students' teachers about what to expect and how to approach teaching the class. I learned that the class would generally have six to nine students in Kindergarten through fifth grade depending on the type of day each student was having. "Melt-downs" or other issues might mean that the student would need a sensory break. I remember wondering, what is sensory? I also learned that I would have help in the class. Two to three paraprofessionals came to music class with the students, which let me breathe a sigh of relief, albeit a small one.

The weekend prior to school starting I was planning the ASD lesson and found myself pulling ideas from every resource I could find: early childhood music, elementary music, instrumental music. My first lesson plan contained enough activities to fill nearly two hours of instructional time as I still had very little idea what to expect in my first 30 minutes with students with autism. I thought it best to be overprepared.

As 9:30 on Thursday morning arrived, I could hear the students and their teachers coming down the hallway. I had pieces of colored craft foam sheets arranged in a small semicircle on the floor, as the circle on the carpet I normally used was far too large for a class of this size. After we got the students seated on their own foam square by using brief, specific directions like, "Alex, sit on green," I began with the Hello song. A few students joined me in keeping the beat, first by patting my knees with my hands and then switching to claps, head nods, and foot stomps. Others just sat with the paraprofessionals and didn't visibly participate. The lesson continued with activities that allowed for many different types of movement, opportunities for individual and group response, and songs and chants in varied meters and tonalities. I was surprised when I looked up at the clock and there were only two minutes remaining. I, and the students, had survived day one.

As the school year progressed, I realized that while developing music lessons for the class of students with autism, I relied heavily on many of the fundamental concepts of early childhood music learning, such as opportunities for reciprocal music communication, talking less (and singing, chanting, and moving more), limiting songs with words, and not forcing or expecting student correctness. I found that lessons adhering to those concepts encouraged students to participate in music class. Additionally, I found that many of the concepts I would use in my class of students with autism were also appropriate for the general education students in grade-level classrooms and began to see more participation and musical reciprocation from the students in those classes as well.

Although my journey into teaching music to students with autism had a rocky start, I now consider it a privilege, and it has made me a better teacher and a better person. It truly was a life-changing experience for me, both professionally and personally. A task that at first seemed daunting became my favorite 30 minutes of the week. Sadly, the autistic program was moved to a different school in my district, and I have also switched to another school. While I'm sad that I no longer teach that class, I am grateful to have had the experience to do so. I, and my teaching, have been changed for the better.

Jim Shouldice
Michigan

Vignette 9.2 is a great example of the importance of overcoming fears by remembering that relying on music education knowledge and techniques that demonstrate good teaching will still resonate as good teaching when presented to a class of students with special needs. This teacher began teaching music to a new population by being resourceful and confident in his musicianship skills and knowledge of child development.

Mr. Shouldice was placed in this situation during his first year of teaching. Many first-year teachers may be placed in similar situations. After speaking to the special educators, Mr. Shouldice began identifying resources that fit the strengths, challenges, and developmental needs of his students. There are many resources listed in chapter 10 and new resources that can be used to meet the communication, social, and sensory needs of students with autism are being designed every day.

Another important idea to take from Mr. Shouldice is the importance of keeping directions simple (using fewer words). This idea is mentioned in chapter 3. Simple, clear directions that accompany an established routine are crucial to success, especially when you are initially assessing and teaching a group of students with autism. Mr. Shouldice also used the first lesson to explore the capabilities of his group. This allowed him to establish a baseline for creating future lessons.

The most important contribution from Mr. Shouldice was his comment "and not forcing or expecting student correctness." Music has many access points. Children with autism are often forced into a box, so to speak. They may not sit in a perfect circle or respond in an appropriate way all the time. They may participate at some times and not others. It is the right and responsibility of music teachers to provide as many opportunities for the child to respond musically as possible and to decide when to remediate (because they know a student can learn the material) or move on (because they know a student has mastered the material even though that evidence is not currently present). The best outcome of this vignette is that Mr. Shouldice realized he already had many tools available to him and that he *was* capable of overcoming the challenges that faced him in this unique environment.

PERFORMANCE-BASED EXAMPLES OF TEACHING MUSIC TO STUDENTS WITH AUTISM

Music performance at the high-school level can be an intimidating and frustrating experience, especially for students with autism. Lights, sound, crowds, scratchy uniforms, waiting your turn, sitting in your seat (before the performance) are all factors to consider. However, the All Access choir

Vignette 9.3
PARTNER CHOIR

For several years, educators at our high school have attempted to integrate special education students into our music classes. Special education students have been welcomed into the band classes to observe and listen. They have worked with music therapists who were brought in from outside the district. Neither of these models, however, fit the needs of our students.

Then, in 2009, I attended an inspiring session at our All-State Music Educators Conference. In front of me stood a side-by-side choir including both general and special education students: in short, a group of "buddies" who worked together to create music and build relationships. This is exactly what we needed! After returning to school, I met with our special education teacher hoping to find some way to include her multi-needs students in our classes.

We initially decided to place several special education students (in this case, students with Down's syndrome and autism) in our Freshman Choir, where they rehearsed with general education freshmen. Unfortunately, this model was frustrating for all of the students. The general education students were frustrated with the groups' inability to uniformly focus on building technique and to learn advanced repertoire. Special education students struggled to find success with the technical demands of the class: not surprisingly, singing in multiple languages and developing a well-blended choral sound were a few of the challenges they faced.

The following school year, we tried again, but this time we more naturally fell into a new model, similar in my mind to the model that so inspired me at the All-State Convention. I began meeting with the special education choral students twice a week during my plan period, along with general education choir student volunteers who had that period free. Within a few weeks, word spread and the class grew to include all of the special education students (about 11 total) and about 15 general education choir students.

By spring, our newest choir was ready for their debut. *All Access*—named by our students—performed in the last two concerts of the school year, receiving standing ovations each time. The group has become the talk of our program. Watching this combination of students work together to create music and build social connections has become the highlight of my day. I can say, without a doubt, that it has had an equally strong impact on both special and general education students. An environment of respect has been created, where students feel safe to take risks in making music.

To date, general education students continue to volunteer their time, and many others are requesting a free period next year so that they can sing with the group. When surveyed, 80% of our choral students have expressed interest in singing with this group during their high school tenure. Though we have accomplished much already in having the group perform at various concerts, there is so little—and inconsistent—time to truly explore the potential of this group. Our vision is to create a curricular class that includes both musical and nonmusical goals (physical, communication, behavioral, emotional and social) for both special and general education students. We have run into some obstacles with funding this course, but are hopeful that our administration will be able to provide support in the near future to provide this quality music education for *all* of our students.

Beth O'Riordan, Downers Grove North High School
Downers Grove, Illinois

is an example of how to provide an opportunity for all students, with and without special needs, to learn. This choir represents the epitome of the inclusion philosophy: students with and without special needs working toward a common goal.

Many students with autism are experiencing transition while they are in high school. They may leave after lunch to attend a job with a coach, or they may be learning a trade at a district-sponsored trade school, with the goal of making a smooth transition into adulthood. These transition opportunities leave little time for socialization and the typical high school experience. Groups like this choir assist with both issues. They allow for socialization and teach all involved the importance of compassion, tolerance and acceptance.

The most important contribution of this piece is the perseverance of Mrs. O'Riordan. In her mind she knew she needed a place for this group of students. Her first attempts were unsuccessful. After reflecting and testing other models, she found one that worked. Her next challenge is to have All Access become a curricular subject at Downers Grove North.

We hope that readers consider this example and create opportunities to incorporate students with special needs into performance-based ensembles. Partner groups are a great start. Many students with special needs could take this instruction and then participate in other performance groups in the community after graduation. Church choirs, community bands, and community orchestras can be places where an adult with autism can connect with the community.

Amy's story is a common one. Many children with disabilities (including autism) are excluded (either by themselves or the organization) from participating in such activities. Her story is positive because the choir director was willing to work with Amy. Often, "we don't have the resources" is a common excuse for excluding children with autism from activities.

Vignette 9.4
AMY

Amy is an 11-year-old who loves to sing and has a lovely voice. She has been diagnosed with mild autism. Amy has an older sister with much more severe disabilities that take much of her mother's attention. Her father does not live with the family. Her mother has been eager to find activities at which Amy can be successful, and music seems to be one of her talents.

Amy has participated for several years in a children's choral summer camp, and has enjoyed it, finding that the children in the camp share many of her interests. This is in contrast with some of her experiences in school, where she often becomes frustrated that other students are unwilling to talk about and do the things she wants to talk about and do. Another positive aspect of the camp is that the counselors (undergraduate music education majors who have had an unusual level of education in working with students with special needs) are enthusiastic and patient, helping Amy to navigate social interactions.

Two years ago, Amy auditioned for and was accepted into the training choir of a large, widely acclaimed community children's choir program. The director, having known Amy's family for several years, was hesitant to accept Amy, as the choir does not have the resources, and not all of the choir staff have the expertise, to serve students with many types of special needs. Amy was accepted with the understanding that the first year would be something of a probationary period. She has done very well musically, but has had difficulty picking up the sometimes subtle social cues, such as when it is and is not appropriate to ask questions, share ideas, move around, and indulge in silliness. She does not understand why other choristers exhibit these behaviors and are met with a positive response, while she sometimes exhibits them and "gets in trouble."

These social and maturity issues have caused Amy to be kept back in the training choir while other choristers her age have been promoted to the more advanced choirs. While she loves singing and performing, she has expressed to her mother and her training choir director that she is not sure she wants to stay with the choir program if she is not promoted next year. Amy's training choir director is hesitant to promote her, partly because the director of the more advanced choirs has little experience and expertise in working with children with special needs, and the musical demands in those choirs do not allow much time to teach and develop social skills.

After meeting with Amy's mother, Amy's director has made a list of behaviors that are a concern and that might be problematic in the advanced choirs. She had met with Amy and talked specifically about each of these behaviors. Together, they have come up with a series of "secret signals" to help Amy know when she is beginning to exhibit an inappropriate behavior. So far, this strategy has been successful, and the behaviors have begun to lessen, giving Amy's director some confidence that Amy may be successful in the more advanced choirs without the signals, and as she continues to mature.

Joy Anderson
Harrisonburg, Virginia

This story also illustrates an additional concern, parent fatigue. It is difficult for someone not involved in the life of a child with autism to understand the tireless effort this parent has had to make by the time Amy has reached this age. It has probably been the same story in every activity. The parent of a child with autism is often called upon to be the child's helper for every activity. There is no dropping Amy off at soccer practice or girl scouts. Every time a new activity begins, the parent is also directly involved.

When music teachers place students with autism in classrooms or settings, it is important to keep parent/family fatigue in mind. By offering a place for the student and also the support the parent and child need to succeed, a music educator is indeed demonstrating inclusiveness. Do not assume anything. For example, most students Amy's age would be dropped off and picked up from a choir rehearsal. Is this safe for Amy? Does the director need to walk Amy to the car? Are there other safety and well-being issues that may need to be addressed for this inclusion to be successful? Parents may also be fatigued from brainstorming situations and solutions. They may also be reticent to ask for more from a group leader who is willing to accept their child because they are already grateful for the inclusive opportunity and do not want to ask for additional assistance. If they are approached with solutions to possible situations, much of the anxiety will dissipate and the family and child will be able to begin the experience knowing that their needs will be met whenever possible.

Jared will benefit from having a buddy accompanying him in hallways. Opening and closing a locker can take quite a while when fine motor skills are weak. This can also lead to bullying and teasing as other students see the weaknesses without understanding the reason for them. When Jared becomes confused or is unable to remember his schedule for the day, or when the sequences he must perform to assemble and disassemble his instrument or prepare for class, a picture schedule or a picture book that delineates each step can help him become more independent. Jared may have difficulty with change. Most middle schools experience change on a daily basis and he will need to become more accepting of change and willing to adapt when unexpected events occur. While he is developing these skills,

Vignette 9.5
JARED

Jared, a sixth grader, was diagnosed with autism at age two. His family noticed differences in Jared's learning from an early age when compared to his older brother. As a baby, Jared did not engage in eye contact with the person speaking to him or respond to his name being called. His eye contact has improved little with age.

As a baby, when Jared should have been babbling as part of language acquisition, he was silent. Language skills were significantly delayed, and he did not speak his first word until age three. He still speaks in a monotonic voice. Jared would at times be fixated on a toy, that is. a specific train car. He would maintain interest only in that object and make repetitive play. Jared would throw tantrums if the object was not in his possession or was held by his brother.

Jared's parents took Jared to their pediatrician, who then referred them to a psychologist and a speech and language specialist. Jared was diagnosed with autism. His parents researched autism to learn about language acquisition, cognitive fixation (attention), and behavior management. Jared was placed in speech therapy at age two.

Currently, Jared is in his first year in middle school. He is learning to change classes, use a locker, and participate in large classes (more than 25 students in general education and 45 in physical education). The transition from elementary to middle school has been difficult. Jared has been lost in the hallways and found hiding in a corner after the hallways have cleared. Learning to open a locker has been frustrating. He does not have patience to attempt opening the lock more than once.

Academically, Jared loses focus in class for many reasons. When he has a rough morning at home, such as a favorite shirt not being clean or there is no more of his favorite cereal for breakfast, he is distracted the entire day. Sometimes Jared hears the whistle of a nearby train passing through town. This distracts him and he fixates on trains for hours, pointing to his notebook that has trains on the cover.

Jared's attention is best when teachers maintain consistent daily procedures. He struggles when teachers are unorganized or activities change without prior notice of at least one day. When an unannounced schedule change occurs, Jared is unproductive for several classes the rest of the day. One example is when a fire alarm sounded. Jared held his hands over his ears and rocked back and forth. The teacher assisted Jared out of the building. Upon returning, Jared was inattentive the rest of the day. Additionally, the teacher learned Jared's sensitivity to noises, despite reviewing class accommodations prior to the start of the year.

Jared is capable of successfully understanding concepts taught in class but often does not complete assignments by the deadline. He requires much teacher redirection to try to stay on task, i.e., listening to the teacher, reading, and completing work. When placed in cooperative learning groups Jared does not participate.

Jared does not communicate well verbally. If he is frustrated with himself or the teacher, Jared growls, eventually walks away, and sits in a quiet place in the classroom.

Socially, Jared has no friends. He does not converse with students, although he can speak short sentences. Students do not know how to respond to Jared's lack of verbal skills and growling. Jared is not bullied, but [he is] generally ignored by other students.

Jared is a member of the Sixth Grade Beginning Band. He is learning to play trombone, the same instrument his father played in high school. During the sixth-grade band recruitment meeting, Jared heard a trombone glissando and decided that would be his instrument.

Sixth-Grade Band meets the last class of the day with forty-two students enrolled. Jared is tardy almost daily due to trying to pack his backpack with books and homework. He must bring his backpack to class since he leaves for the bus from band. When Jared arrives in class, he is usually distracted from being tardy. He waits until no one is near his instrument storage shelf before picking up his trombone. Jared keeps his music on the storage shelf although he has been assigned a place for music storage. His music book is torn from being on the shelf. After picking up his music and instrument, Jared tries to weave between rows to find his seat still with his backpack. Once seated, Jared tries to negotiate the space to assemble his trombone. He is always the last person ready to play.

In band class Jared rarely initiates conversation with the band director or students. He does not ask for help when needed and does not like to answer teacher-directed questions.

Jared enjoys playing trombone, especially glissandos. He has a natural embouchure and a good beginning tone. A challenge is reading the notes. Jared, who has high melodic aptitude, plays more by ear than from reading notes in the book. He memorizes the exercises while other students are still learning notes.

At the end of class, Jared has to disassemble his instrument, place music in his backpack, and be ready when the bell rings to catch his bus. Jared has missed the bus several times this year.

Dr. Susan Harvey
Midwestern State University

ample notice regarding school assemblies, fire drills, and other changes to the day's routine may be incredibly helpful.

Including Jared in this busy middle-school environment will be most effective if the inclusion is addressed via a team approach. In the class prior to band, Jared will benefit from having his teacher assist him as he prepares to leave the classroom and walk to band. It will be important socially for Jared to arrive at band on time. One of his teachers, or a student (buddy) may assist in organizing assignments for Jared to take home. When Jared returns to his locker, those assignments can be placed on one shelf. Jared will probably need a homework notebook/folder that goes to all classes and he will need his teachers to help place those assignments in his notebook/folder. If this team approach is followed, all assignments, notices from teachers, and information will be together for his family to see when Jared arrives home from school.

Many considerations will need to be made to assist Jared when participating cooperatively in band and so that he is able to engage in social situations with other students. If Jared has a rotating buddy within the trombone section, his buddies can take turns assisting him academically and socially. When Jared is able to perform a portion of music well, enthusiastic, positive expressions of approval will increase the possibility that he will repeat those positive academic behaviors.

Jared will benefit from a clear, established routine for all students. If his materials (backpack, music, trombone case) are placed in a set place each day, Jared will be able to learn how to retrieve them at the end of band class. He may need to sit in his chair and then have his buddies put his materials in the assigned place while he prepares for class.

Preferential seating will be necessary for Jared. If he sits at the end of his section, he will not be as affected by the loud sounds, and no sound will be coming from behind him to serve as a possible distraction. When providing instruction and assessment, a multimodal approach will be the most effective in this situation. Jared will need processing time and a choice of response methods to demonstrate understanding. The band director may also choose to work with Jared's speech and language therapist to add the words Jared knows to rhythmic and melodic patterns. This can help Jared create his own meaning from rhythms and melodic patterns that he can share to demonstrate competency. It will also reinforce language acquisition and help Jared speak in a less monotonic voice.

The planning and implementation of accommodations and modification for Jared will be considerable, however, they will greatly increase the amount of time the band director will be able to spend teaching and rehearsing once the year begins. Jared, and the other band members, will benefit from the inclusive and cooperative environment. The end result is a better learning environment for all.

Vignette 9.6
ALEX

Alex is a fifth grader with autism. He has a few words; however, for the most part he can let you know what he needs or use short phrases to tell his friends about his favorite things. His paraprofessional would describe him as very engaging.

Mrs. Anderson welcomed Alex into music class and requested that the class sit in a circle around the piano. She began her hello song. Alex uses a variety of manipulatives to soothe some of his sensory needs. One of them is a small plastic slinky. Alex was participating as well as he could; however, at the same time he was flipping his slinky around in front of his face. Mrs. Anderson tells Alex to stop because it is distracting the other students. Obviously, because Alex is limited in his communication, he did not understand her.

Out of frustration, Mrs. Anderson takes the slinky away from Alex and tells him he can have it after class. Alex begins the meltdown of a lifetime resulting in him taking off his pants in protest. The paraprofessional helped him get dressed and took him out of the room.

Because she was embarrassed, Mrs. Anderson did not say anything to her supervisors. Alex's parents found out about this incident through "the grapevine" and immediately called the principal concerned about the goings on in Mrs. Anderson's class. Had other incidents occurred without notifying the student's parents?

Students with autism often have sensory needs. These are real needs that must be met for the student to be able to learn. Alex has a sensory "diet" (manipulatives, etc.) that helps him remain focused and calm during class. When Mrs. Anderson abruptly removed the sensory item, Alex had no other way to express his anxiety and frustration. His only way to indicate that he was extremely upset was to scream, cry, and remove his pants. The drastic measures he took mirrored the way he felt inside when his sensory item was taken away.

Alex had a paraprofessional in the room. The paraprofessional had not been given any direction or instruction from the music teacher and did not see herself as being empowered to step in on behalf of Alex. When a paraprofessional is available and in the music classroom, it is an opportunity for the music teacher to learn about the student, his needs, and to utilize the paraprofessional during instruction time. Had the communication between the paraprofessional and music educator been open and ongoing, this situation may have never occurred.

Vignette 9.7
LESLIE

As a teacher of kids with special needs in an autism classroom, I have learned that advocating for my students is, first and foremost, one of my main responsibilities and also a daily necessity. When working with teachers of music, art or P.E., sometimes uncertainty or misunderstandings can arise, and many times these are simply instances of a lack of communication between the general education (music) teacher and the classroom teacher (special education teacher). I find that consistent communication and remaining proactive in your approaches are necessary to help with the growth of the students' experiences in those particular classes.

Open communication is the most proactive and beneficial thing for all professionals and students involved in any classroom setting. It's important that the general education (music) teacher express any concerns they come across in their classroom so that they can work together to resolve conflicts or perplexities that may arise. One thing the general education (music) teacher should take care to remember is that they only see the students for a short amount of time compared to the classroom teacher, therefore it is important to work closely together and keep those lines of communication open.

Open minds are also some of the best tools that teachers can have. One part of my responsibility to the other teachers in the building is being sure to get them my students' individual goals. Another perhaps more crucial responsibility of the special education teacher is to help get the materials, training and resources to the general education (music) teacher to help them better understand how to educate my students in the most efficient way. I believe the goal in every situation in teaching is to be proactive; to be able to foresee potential distracters or problems and stop them before they occur.

It is helpful for both the classroom teacher and the fine arts teacher to understand one important idea: each teacher has specific and highly effective knowledge and training that the other does not possess. This is where being open-minded comes into play as well—as a special education teacher, it is my duty to provide behavioral, sensory, and social suggestions—not to tell others what to teach, [but] rather how the students will have a better experience in their class. In fact, one recommendation I have for teachers is to find time to go observe the students with special needs in a classroom setting where they feel conformable and have the structure that is vital to help them be successful. When the principles of openness, and mutual respect and consideration are applied, both professionals benefit from the experience.

Leah Sullenbarger
Storer Elementary School, Muncie, Indiana

Understanding the sensory needs of a student with autism is critical. Understanding the relationship with the paraprofessionals and others who work with students with autism is also critical to success. The ability of a music educator to become knowledgeable about the students she teaches as well as others who work with those students, particularly students with special needs, is an essential part of the music education profession. Without this knowledge, well-developed relationships, and a sense of compassion on the part of music educators, students with limited communication skills will feel the need to express their frustration in any way they are able.

The importance of music educators to communicate with other professionals, as noted in several of the case studies, cannot be overstated. By building relationships and working as a member of the team, the music educator not only helps enhance the quality of education received by her students, she is also advocating for the importance of music education in the curriculum. Many students with autism find success in the music classroom. Building on these successes can create leisure skills that can be utilized throughout their lives (in church or community choirs, bands, orchestras, or more informal music-making opportunities).

As a part of creating relationships with other professionals, observing students in other classes (general, special, and fine arts) can create partnerships in behavioral, communication, and sensorial plans for students with autism. These observations can also lead to further collaboration opportunities between professionals in a school or school district. For further specific information regarding these types of observations, it is recommended that you read chapter 3 of *Teaching Music to Students with Special Needs: A Label-Free Approach*.

CONCLUSION

We hope that this chapter provided a real-life snapshot of circumstances that exist in public-school settings. The aim is to provide a balance of best practice and practical ideas to enhance day-to-day teaching strategies. There are some common threads to emphasize: first, open communication among all the parties involved is the best circumstance possible for a student with autism. With communication comes consistency. This is also essential for students on the spectrum.

Second, music teachers must not assume anything about the skills of a student with autism. Just because they are not able to communicate verbally does not mean they cannot communicate musically (and the converse). It is important to spend some time establishing a baseline of understanding by observing the student and talking with other teachers.

Finally, advocating for a student with autism is very important. Many of these students have difficulty advocating for themselves. The best way to advocate for a student with autism is to make sure they are placed in a musical environment where they can be successful. This may mean thinking "outside the box" and deriving new ways to teach music as well as new groupings of students to provide the true least restrictive environment for all.

CHAPTER 10

Resources for Music Teachers

INTERNET RESOURCES
Internet Resources Pertaining to Persons with Autism

The Ability Project: Autism
http://www.ability.org.uk.autism.html

This portion of the Ability Project's site is an extensive list of Internet links related to Autism International; state autism organizations and societies are included, as well as a wide variety of sites with information, advocacy and policies related to autism. Sites are listed in alphabetical order, not by category.

Autism One International
http://www.autismone.org

Website of Autism One, a nonprofit, charity organization started by a small group of parents of children with autism. The website offers an online support community as well as videos, blogs, forums, research, and media coverage pertaining to autism.

Autism Research Institute
http://www.autism.com/ari/

Website of Autism Research Institute (ARI), a worldwide network of parents and professionals concerned with autism. Founded in 1967, ARI aims to conduct and foster scientific research designed to improve the methods of diagnosing, treating, and preventing autism. ARI also disseminates research findings to parents and others seeking help worldwide. The ARI data bank, the world's largest, contains over 40,000 detailed case histories of autistic children from over 60 countries. ARI publishes the *Autism Research Review*

International, a quarterly newsletter covering biomedical and educational advances in autism research. The site provides a wealth of information specifically intended for families, teachers, providers, and ASD individuals.

> AutismHelp.org
> http://autismhelp.info/default.aspx

Autism Help aims to increase awareness of ASD through practical strategies listed by specific developmental level: early childhood, primary years, teen years and adult years. The website resources are for parents, teachers, child-care workers, and professionals in the field.

> Autism Society of America
> http://www.autism-society.org

The Autism Society of America (ASA) is a grassroots organization that seeks to improve the lives of everyone affected by autism. Their website includes practical information on autism and living with autism as well as research and news on autism.

> Autism Speaks
> http://www.autismspeaks.org/

Website of one of the nation's largest autism science and advocacy organizations, dedicated to funding research into the causes, prevention, treatments, and a cure for autism; increasing awareness of ASDs; and advocating for the needs of individuals with autism and their families. Autism Speaks' website offers helpful information about autism, science, advocacy, family resources, and autism news. Apps for autism are listed with explanations of each. Specific sections pertaining to the specific challenges of PDD-NOS and Asperger syndrome are found on the site. It is also available in Spanish.

> The National Autism Association
> http://www.nationalautismassociation.org

Website of the National Autism Association, a national organization whose goal is to respond to the most urgent needs of the autism community by providing help and hope. The website offers resources on specific needs and challenges associated with autism. Information on membership and local chapters is included.

The National Autistic Society
http://www.nas.org/uk/

Website of a large charity based in the United Kingdom for people with autism (including Asperger syndrome) and their families. Includes extensive information on diagnosis, living with autism, intervention, social care, community care, support and and education. News, media, and information on conferences are available on the website.

Help with Autism, Asperger Syndrome & Related Disorders
http://www.autism-help.org/

This site offers over 350 fact sheets about autism and autism-related disorders. It emphasizes practical strategies for families that cannot afford expensive interventions or may be geographically isolated.

AAPC Publishing
http://www.aapcpublishing.net/

AAPC Publishing Company specializes in providing information regarding autism spectrum disorders to parents and educators. The books and multimedia that they publish are more practical than technical and address the issues from many different angles.

Future Horizons Inc.
http://www.fhautism.com/

Future Horizons was created to help educators, therapists, and families who face challenges associated with autism and ASDs. They provide books, videos, and conferences that emphasize the most current information for dealing these challenges.

Center for Autism and Related Disorders
http://www.centerforautism.com/

The Center for Autism and Related Disorders (CARD) is an international organization focused on treating children with autism, Asperger syndrome, PDD-NOS, and related disorders. The website offers historical information on the CARD approach and details of their services, including individualized treatment plans. Parent resources, including a glossary, media guide, and information on education rights, are offered.

US Autism & Asperger Association
http://www.usautism.org/

The website for the US Autism & Asperger Association (USAAA), a nonprofit organization for education, support, and solutions. Their goal is to provide the opportunity for individuals with autism spectrum disorders to achieve their fullest potential. USAAA provides research, education, support and solutions through conferences, newsletters and resources, including this website.

Online Autism Communities

Autism Blogger
http://autism-blog.com/

Autism Blogger is a blog community for anyone affected by autism. The site offers free, individual blogs and profiles and is intended to be a space for members to provide mutual help and support.

TheAutSpot.com
http://www.theautspot.com

The AutSpot.com is a free online community that links parents and specialists faced with the challenges of autism. This site offers information and resources on autism, including blogs, online groups and forums, inspirational stories, and a national events calendar.

Talk About Curing Autism
http://www.tacanow.org/about-taca/

Talk About Curing Autism (TACA) is a national nonprofit 501(c)(3) organization that aims to educate, empower and support families affected by autism. For families who have just received the autism diagnosis, TACA aims to speed up the cycle time from the diagnosis to effective treatment. TACA helps to strengthen the autism community by connecting families and the professionals who can help them. The site offers information on TACA and its history, information about autism, volunteer opportunities, and family resources.

AutismSupportNetwork.com
http://www.autismsupportnetwork.com/

The Autism Support Network connects families and individuals touched by ASD with each other, provides support and insight, and acts as a resource guide for education, treatments, strategies, and therapies. The site offers an e-mail newsletter subscription, a support community, resources, events, and news.

Autism Apps

Apps for Autism
https://autismapps.wikispaces.com/

This website is a wiki for sharing autism apps. Membership to these pages require contacting the creator and writing about yourself and why you are interested in participating. Each app is listed by category and described in full, allowing the user to compare and contrast apps easily. Some of the app categories are Word Learning, Books and Literacy, Sensory and Motor Development and Behavior Management.

Hearty SPIN (Solutions for People in Need)
http://heartyspin.com/autism-apps/

Solutions for People in Need (SPIN) is a social enterprise that creates assistive technology solutions and apps that help individuals with special needs and disabilities cope with their daily challenges. One of their developments, "Picture AAC," is an intuitive form of visual communication using pictures for use with iPad, iPhone, and iTouch devices. Picture AAC is suitable for speech-impaired or delayed children and adults with autism or others who are nonverbal or have little functional speech. This website includes features, instructions and testimonials for Picture AAC.

Touch Autism
http://touchautism.com/

Touch Autism is a company dedicated to creating technological apps for autism and other special needs. Their website includes explanations and features of their apps. Touch Autism apps include Turn Taker, Calm Counter, Preference Assessment, and Touch Trainer.

Internet Resources Pertaining to Persons with Asperger Syndrome

Asperger Syndrome Education Network
http://www.aspennj.org/

The website of ASPEN, a national volunteer nonprofit organization that provides individuals and families affected by Asperger syndrome and other

ASDs with education, support, and advocacy. Media, news and recommended reading are included. The website includes links to ASPEN chapters and membership information.

> Families of Adults Affected by Asperger Syndrome (FAAAS, Inc.)
> http://faaas.org/

The goal of FAAAS is to offer support and reassurance to the family members of adult individuals with Asperger syndrome and bring awareness to the existence of this neurological disorder in the adult population. The website includes research materials, articles, services, news and an online community.

> Oasis @ MAAP
> http://aspergersyndrome.org/

A resource of the Online Asperger Syndrome Information and Support (OASIS) Center and MAAP Services for Autism and Asperger Syndrome. The website is intended for families, individuals, and medical professionals who deal with the challenges of Asperger syndrome, autism, and pervasive developmental disorder not otherwise specified (PDD-NOS). The website provides articles, educational resources, links to local, national and international support groups, sources of professional help, lists of camps and schools, conference information, recommended reading, and moderated support message boards. The website resources are an addition to the annual conference, newsletter, and e-mail and phone support provided by MAAP Services.

Internet Resources Pertaining to Persons with Rett Syndrome

> International Rett Syndrome Foundation (IRSF)
> http://www.rettsyndrome.org/

Website of the International Rett Syndrome Foundation. The core mission of the IRSF is to fund research for treatments and a cure for Rett syndrome while enhancing the overall quality of life for those living with Rett syndrome by providing information, programs, and services. This comprehensive website offers general information about Rett syndrome while also providing extensive information about research. Helpful information is given for families including practical living tips, communication aids, educational assistance and new diagnosis information. Several online communities are listed, including support groups, a "Life after Rett" Facebook support group and "The RettNet," which is a moderated e-mail list-serve forum for all interested persons who wish to openly discuss the many facets of Rett syndrome. Volunteer and fundraising information is provided, as well as a section of current events and conference information.

Rett Syndrome Research Trust (RSRT)
http://www.rsrt.org/

Launched in 2008, the RSRT exists to find a cure for Rett Syndrome and related genetic disorders. The RSRT is not a grant-making organization, but one that seeks to identify, catalyze, evaluate, prioritize, support, and monitor research projects. The website includes detailed information on the RSRT's current projects as well as general information about Rett syndrome. Special attention is given to new diagnoses, the education of a child with Rett syndrome and available workshops and clinics.

Rett.com
http://www.Rett.com/

Rett.com was developed by parents of children with Rett syndrome. The underlying belief of the site developers is that people with Rett syndrome can live remarkable lives, particularly when provided with the opportunities, tools, and training to overcome their physical disabilities. The focus of the site is support and assistance for families of children with Rett syndrome. Simple explanations of Rett syndrome's cause, symptoms and diagnosis are balanced with members' posts and media information. Member posts are archived can be found within many categories such as advocacy, diagnosis, education, "Rett Dads," "Rett Moms," and treatment.

Rett TV
http://rett.tv/

This website is a comprehensive listing of internet videos pertaining to Rett syndrome. The site organizers report conducting daily searches to retrieve videos from the internet, but anyone may submit videos for posting free of charge. Video content includes media features, personal stories, therapy, and advocacy.

PRINT RESOURCES FOR MUSIC EDUCATORS AND MUSIC TEACHER EDUCATORS

Research within Music Education Pertaining to Students with Autism

Allen, R., Heaton, P., & Hill, E. (2009). "Hath charms to soothe...": An exploratory study of how high functioning adults with ASD experience music. *International Journal of Research and Practice, 13*(1), 21–41.

Allen, R., & Heaton, P. (2010). Autism, music, and the therapeutic potential of music in alexithymia. *Music Perception: An Interdisciplinary Journal, 27*(4), 251–261.

Allgood, N. (2005). Parents' perceptions of family-based group music therapy for children with autism spectrum disorders. *Music Therapy Perspectives, 23*(2), 92–99.

Bakan, M. B., Koen, B. D., Bakan, M., Kobylarz, F., Morgan, L., Goff, R., & Kahn, S. (2008). Saying something else: Improvisation and music-play facilitation in a medical ethnomusicology program for children on the autism spectrum. *College Music Symposium, 48*, 1–30.

Graham, G. (2001). Music and autism. *Journal of Aesthetic Education, 35*(2), 39–47.

Greher, G. R., Hillier, A., Dougherty, M., & Nataliya, P. (2010). SoundScape: An interdisciplinary music intervention for adolescents and young adults on the autism spectrum. *International Journal of Education & the Arts, 11*(9). Retrieved March 5, 2013, http://www.ijea.org/v11n9/v11n9/pdf.

Heaton, P., Allen, R., Williams, K., Cummins, O., Happe, F. (2008). Do social and cognitive deficits curtail musical understanding? Evidence from autism and Down syndrome. *British Journal of Developmental Psychology, 26*(2), 171–182.

Kaplan, R. (2004). Music therapy, sensory integration and the autistic child. *Music Therapy Perspectives, 22*(1), 56–58.

Kaplan, R. S. (2005). An analysis of music therapy program goals and outcomes for clients with diagnoses on the autism spectrum. *Journal of Music Therapy, 42*(1), 2–19.

Kaplan, R. (2008). Book review. Music therapy group work with special needs children: the evolving process, by K. D. Goodman. *Journal of Music Therapy, 45*(4), 507–511.

Katagiri, J. (2009). The effect of background music and song texts on the emotional understanding of children with autism. *Journal of Music Therapy, 46*(1), 15–31.

Kern, P. (2007). Improving the performance of a young child with autism during self-care tasks using embedded song interventions: A case study. *Music Therapy Perspectives, 25*(1), 43–51.

Lanovaz, M. J., Sladeczek, I. E., & Rapp, J. T. (2011). Effects of music on stereotyping children with autism. *Journal of Applied Behavior Analysis, 44*(3), 647–651.

McCord, K. (2009). Improvisation as communication: Students with communication disabilities and autism using call and responses on instruments. *Australian Journal of Music Education, 2*, 17–26.

Paciello, M. (2003). Book review. Music therapy, sensory integration and the autistic child, by Dorita S. Berger. *British Journal of Music Education, 20*(1), 112–115.

Pasiali, V. (2004). The use of prescriptive therapeutic songs in a home-based environment to promote social skills acquisition by children with autism: Three case studies. *Music Therapy Perspectives, 22*(1), 11–20.

Simpson, K., & Keen, D. (2011). Music interventions for children with autism: Narrative review of the literature. *Journal of Autism and Developmental Disorders, 41*(11), 1507–1514.

Walworth, D. D. (2007). The use of music therapy within the SCERTS model for children with autism spectrum disorder. *Journal of Music Therapy, 44*(1), 2–22.

Whipple, J. (2004). Music in intervention for children and adolescents with autism: A meta-analysis. *Journal of Music Therapy, 41*(2), 90.

Dissertations within Music Education
and Music Therapy

Barnes, J. P. (2010). *Moments of meeting: Difficulties and developments in shared attention, inter-action, and communication with children with autism during two years of music therapy in a public preschool class.* Available from ProQuest Dissertations and Theses database. (UMI No. 3449507)

Bhatara, A. K. (2008). *Music as a means of investigating perception of emotion and social attri-bution in typical development and in autism spectrum disorders.* Available from ProQuest Dissertations and Theses database. (UMI No. NR66631)

Carpente, J. A. (2009). *Contributions of Nordoff-Robbins music therapy within a developmental, individual-differences, relationship-based (DIRRTM)/floortime framework to the treatment of children with autism: Four case studies.* Available from ProQuest Dissertations and Theses database. (UMI No. 3359621)

Chou, Y. (2008). *The effect of music therapy and peer-mediated interventions on social-communicative responses of children with autism spectrum disorders.* Available from ProQuest Dissertations and Theses database. (UMI 1459803)

DeVito, D. (2006). *The communicative function of behavioral responses to music by public school students with autism spectrum disorder.* Available from ProQuest Dissertations and Theses database. (UMI No. 3224531)

Duffy, V. A. (2012). *Musical social stories and the preschool child with autism spectrum disorder.* Available from ProQuest Dissertations and Theses database. (UMI No. 3504191)

Fang, E. R. (2010). *Music in the lives of two children with autism: A case study.* Available from ProQuest Dissertations and Theses database. (UMI No. 1473522)

Gitman, K. (2010). *The effects of music therapy on children and adolescents with mental or medi-cal illness: A meta-analysis.* Available from ProQuest Dissertations and Theses database. (UMI No. 3407897)

Griffith, C. (2009). *Examining experiences of teaching music to a child with autism while using a music learning theory-based intervention during informal music sessions infused with DIR/Floortime strategies.* Available from ProQuest Dissertations and Theses database. (UMI No. 1463997)

Houtaling, C. M. (2003). *Music and Rett syndrome: A survey from the parental perspective.* Available from ProQuest Dissertations and Theses database. (UMI No. 1414651)

Joseph, C. (2011). *Integrating music education, music therapy and special education in a music classroom.* Available from ProQuest Dissertations and Theses database. (UMI No. 3475951)

O'Loughlin, R. A. (2000). *Facilitating prelinguistic communication skills of attention by integrating a music stimulus within typical language intervention with autistic children.* Available from ProQuest Dissertations and Theses database. (UMI No. 9965033)

Partington, M. R. (2010). *Social stories as songs: The combination of music therapy and social sto-ries for a treatment intervention for children with autism spectrum disorders.* Available from ProQuest Dissertations and Theses database. (UMI No. 3436696)

Reschke-Hernandez, A. (2010). *Evaluation of a developmentally-based music therapy assessment tool for children with autism.* Available from ProQuest Dissertations and Theses database. (UMI No. 1484163)

Ropp, C. R. (2008). *Special education administrators' perceptions of music therapy: A national perspective.* Available from ProQuest Dissertations and Theses database. (UMI No. 3353094)

Seagren, S. (2009). *An examination of music therapy with adolescent populations.* Available from ProQuest Dissertations and Theses database. (UMI No. 1465053)

Stanutz, S. (2009). *Pitch discrimination and melodic memory in children with autism.* Available from ProQuest Dissertations and Theses database. (UMI No. NR66536)

Tindell, K. W. (2010). *Comparison of music-based curriculum versus an eclectic curriculum for speech acquisition in students with autism spectrum disorder.* Available from ProQuest Dissertations and Theses database. (UMI No. 3413582)

Webb, K. (2009). *Does change in timbre alter stereotypy movements exhibited by three persons with diagnoses of mental retardation and autism spectrum disorder: Three case studies.* Available from ProQuest Dissertations and Theses database. (UMI No. 3383765)

Yoo, G. (2010). *The effect of musical attention cues on the frequency and accuracy of joint attention behaviors of children with autism.* Available from ProQuest Dissertations and Theses database. (UMI No. 1477240)

Books within Music Therapy and Music Education

Berger, D. S. (2002). *Music therapy, sensory integration, and the autistic child.* London: Jessica Kingsley Publishers.

Brunk, B. K. (2004). *Music therapy: Another path to learning and communication for children on the autism spectrum.* Arlington, TX: Future Horizons.

Grandin, T. (2008). *The way I see it: A personal look at autism and Asperger's.* Arlington, TX: Future Horizons.

Lewis, C. (2008). *Rex: A mother, her autistic child, and the music that transformed their lives.* Nashville, TN: Thomas Nelson.

Lim, H. A. (2010). *Developmental speech-language training through music for children with autism spectrum disorders: Theory and clinical application.* London: Jessica Kinsley Publishers.

Lloyd, P. (2008). *Let's all listen: Songs for group work in settings that include students with learning difficulties and autism.* London: Jessica Kingsley.

Ruben, S. (2004). *Awakening Ashley: Mozart knocks autism on its ear.* New York: IUniverse.

Tubbs, J. (2008). *Creative therapy for children with autism, ADD, and Asperger's: Using artistic creativity to reach, teach, and touch our children.* Garden City Park, NY: Square One Publishers.

Books within General Education

Anderson, S. R. (2007). *Self-help skills for people with autism: A systematic teaching approach.* Bethesda, MD: Woodbine House.

Ben-Arieh, J. (2009). *The educator's guide to teaching students with autism spectrum disorders.* Thousand Oaks, CA: Corwin Press.

Berkell, Z. D., Wehmeyer, M. L., & Simpson, R. L., eds. (2012). *Educating students with autism spectrum disorders: Research-based principles and practices.* New York: Routledge.

De Boer, S. R. (2009). *Successful inclusion for students with autism: Creating a complete, effective ASD inclusion program.* San Francisco, CA: Jossey-Bass.

Cimera, R. E. (2007). *Making autism a gift: Inspiring children to believe in themselves and lead happy, fulfilling lives.* Lanham, MD: Rowman & Littlefield.

Harris, S. L., & Weiss, M. J. (2007). *Right from the start: Behavioral intervention for young children with autism* (2nd ed.). Bethesda, MD: Woodbine House.

Holzhauser-Peters, L. (2008). *Making sense of children's thinking and behavior: A step by step tool for understanding children diagnosed with NLD, Asperger's, HFA, PDD- NOS, and other neurological differences.* London: Jessica Kingsley Publishers.

Ilona, R. (2010). *The autism spectrum in the 21st century: Exploring psychology, biology and practice.* London: Jessica Kingsley Publishers.

Kluth, P. (2003). *"You're going to love this kid": Teaching students with autism in the inclusive classroom.* Baltimore, MD: P.H. Brookes.

Koegel, L. K., & LaZebnik, C. S. (2004). *Overcoming autism.* New York: Viking.

Leach, D. (2010). *Bringing ABA into your inclusive classroom: A guide to improving outcomes for students with autism spectrum disorders.* Baltimore. MD: Paul H. Brookes.

Lewis, J. & Wilson, D. (1998). *Pathways to learning in Rett syndrome.* London: David Fulton Publishers.

Lindberg, B. (1994). *Understanding Rett syndrome: A practical guide for parents, teachers, and therapists.* Cambridge: Hogrefe Publishing.

Notbohm, E., & Zysk, V. (2004). *1001 great ideas for teaching and raising children with autism spectrum disorders.* Arlington, TX: Future Horizons.

Sicile-Kira, C. (2004). *Autism spectrum disorders: The complete guide to understanding autism, Asperger's syndrome, pervasive developmental disorder, and other ASDs.* New York: Perigee.

Siegel, B. (2003). *Helping children with autism learn: Treatment approaches for parents and professionals.* London: Oxford.

Wagner, S. (2009). *Inclusive programming for high school students with autism or Asperger's syndrome.* Arlington, TX: Future Horizons.

Wilkinson, L. A. (2010). *A best practice guide to assessment and intervention for autism and Asperger syndrome in schools.* London: Jessica Kingsley Publishers.

Williams, B. F., & Williams, R. L. (2011). *Effective programs for treating autism spectrum disorder: Applied behavior analysis models.* New York: Routledge.

Practitioner Articles within Music Education

Allgood, N. (2005). Parents' perceptions of family-based group music therapy for children with autism spectrum disorders. *Music Therapy Perspectives, 23*(2), 92–99.

Armstrong, T. (1999). Research on music and autism: Implications for music educators. *Update: Applications of Research in Music Education, 18*(1), 15–20.

Au, S. (2003). Principal themes: Musical interaction with autistic and multiple-handicapped children. *Canadian Music Educator, 45*(1), 19–21.

Cannon, M. C. (2008). Teaching and learning: Working with the autistic student. *American Suzuki Journal, 36*(3), 32–33.

Darrow, A.-A. (2009). Adapting for students with autism. *General Music Today, 22*(2), 24–26.

Darrow, A.-A., & Armstrong, T. (1999). Research on music and autism: Implications for music educators. *Update: Applications of Research in Music Education, 18*(1), 15–20.

Hagedorn, V. S. (2003). Special learners: Using picture books in music class to encourage participation of students with autistic spectrum disorder. *General Music Today (online), 17*(2), 46–51.

Hourigan, R., & Hourigan, A. (2009). Teaching music to children with autism: Understandings and perspectives. *Music Educators Journal, 96*(1), 40–45.

Iseminger, S. H. (2009). Keys to success with autistic children. *Teaching Music, 16*(6), 28–31.

Kaplan, R. (2004). Music therapy, sensory integration and the autistic child. *Music Therapy Perspectives, 22*(1), 56–58.

Kaplan, R. S. (2005). An analysis of music therapy program goals and outcomes for clients with diagnoses on the autism spectrum. *Journal of Music Therapy, 42*(1), 2–19.

Katagiri, J. (2009). The effect of background music and song texts on the emotional understandings of children with autism. *Journal of Music Therapy, 46*(1), 15–31.

Kern, P. (2006). Using embedded music therapy interventions to support outdoor play of young children with autism in an inclusive community-based child care program. *Journal of Music Therapy, 43*(4), 270–294.

Kern. P. (2007). Improving the performance of a young child with autism during self-care tasks using embedded song interventions: A case study. *Music Therapy Perspectives, 25*(1), 43–51.

Kim, J., Wigram, T., & Gold, C. (2009). Emotional, motivational and interpersonal responsiveness of children with autism in improvisational music therapy. *Autism: The International Journal of Research and Practice, 13*(4), 389–409.

McCord, K. (2009). Improvisation as communication: Students with communication disabilities and autism using call and response on instruments. *Australian Journal of Music Education, 2,* 17–26.

Walworth, D. D. (2007). The use of music therapy within the scerts model for children with autism spectrum disorder. *Journal of Music Therapy, 44*(1), 2–22.

Dr. Alice M. Hammel, a leader in the field of teaching music to students with special needs, currently teaches for James Madison and Virginia Commonwealth Universities. Her background in the field of music education is extensive and includes teaching and research with students in preschool through postgraduate school. Her degrees are from the Florida State University (MME) and Shenandoah University (DMA and BME—magna cum laude). Dr. Hammel holds Level III Kodály Certification from James Madison University.

Pursuing a lifelong interest in the needs of students with special needs, Dr. Hammel has presented her research at many state and national conferences. Her research focus is the adaptation of methods and materials for students with special needs, learning styles, and teacher education and preparation. She has published widely, and was a member of the editorial board of the *Journal for Music Teacher Education*. Articles based on her research have been published by the *Music Educators Journal; UPDATE: Applications of Research in Music Education; Journal for Music Teacher Education; Arts Education Policy Review University Affiliated Programs in Developmental Disabilities; American Music Teacher; Keyboard Companion; Massachusetts Music News;* and *Virginia Music Educators Association—Notes*. She is a contributing author to two resources available through NAfME—*Spotlight on Teaching Special Learners* and *Readings in Diversity, Inclusion, and Music for All*. An online and CD-ROM-supported course co-authored by Dr. Hammel, *On Music for Special Learners*, is available through Connect for Education. Drs. Hammel and Hourigan co-authored *Teaching Music to Students with Special Needs: A Label-Free Approach* (2011). Dr. Hammel is Students with Special Needs Chair for the Virginia Music Educators Association.

Dr. Hammel is also active as a professional flutist and maintains an independent flute studio. She has participated in numerous national panel presentations regarding woodwind pedagogy and learning styles. She is a nationally known adjudicator and clinician for solo wind, band, orchestra, and choral competitions, and frequently conducts master classes and presents lectures throughout the United States. Dr. Hammel was Wind Representative to the Pedagogy Board of the Music Teachers National Association for four years and has served as Chair of Single-Line Sight Reading for the Virginia Music Teachers Association. She can be heard as a flutist on two compact discs of music composed by Allan Blank (published by Arizona State Recordings and Centaur Recordings).

Dr. Hammel is a multiple recipient of awards honoring her commitment to music education and the inclusion of all students in music classrooms, including the 2000 Young Career Achievement Award by Shenandoah University, and is a frequent keynote speaker for events in the areas of education and students with special needs. Dr. Hammel is a member of the National Association for Music Education (formerly MENC), Society for Music Teacher Education, Music Teachers National Association, the Association for Supervision and Curriculum Development, Sigma Alpha Iota, the Organization of American Kodály Educators, and The Council for Exceptional Children. She is married to Dr. Bruce Hammel. They have two daughters, Hannah and Hollie.

Dr. Ryan M. Hourigan (2010 Indiana Music Educators Association University Music Educator of the Year) joined the faculty at Ball State University in fall 2006 after nine years of teaching instrumental and vocal music at the secondary and university levels. A native of Illinois, Dr. Hourigan holds degrees from Eastern Illinois University (BM), Michigan State University (MM Wind Conducting), and a PhD in Music Education from the University of Michigan.

Dr. Hourigan teaches instrumental music education and is Associate Director of the School of Music at Ball State University. His research interests include the preparation of preservice music teachers, music students with special needs, professional development for music teachers, and preservice music teacher identity development. Dr. Hourigan has been published or is in press in *Journal of Research in Music Education*; *Update: Applications of Research in Music Education*; *Arts Education Policy Review*; *Journal of Music Teacher Education*; *Music Educators Journal*; *and Bulletin for the Council of Research in Music Education*. In 2007, His dissertation, entitled "Teaching Music to Students with Special Needs: A Phenomenological Examination of Participants in a Fieldwork Experience," won the national dissertation award from Council for Research in Music Education.

In 2009, Dr. Hourigan founded the Prism Project. This program provides an opportunity for Ball State students to gain skills in the area of teaching students with special needs. Every spring, the members of the Prism Project present a capstone performance highlighting scenes and music created through a collaborative effort between the Ball State volunteers and the 20 performers with special needs. There is a detailed documentary of the project including student and instructor interviews at http://prismproject.iweb.bsu.edu.

Dr. Hourigan has presented at state and national conferences including the American Educational Research Association (AERA) and the Music Educators National Conference. Dr. Hourigan is a member of the American Educational Research Association (AERA), College Music Society (CMS), Music Educators National Conference (MENC), the Society for Music Teacher Education (SMTE), and Phi Mu Alpha Sinfonia. Dr. Hourigan lives in Muncie, Indiana, with his wife Amy and his two sons, Joshua and Andrew.

INDEX

Affective development
Administrative Support 22
Asperger syndrome 2, 3, 148–152, 157
Augmentative and Alternative
    Communication 45
Autism Society of America 2, 126, 148
Autism Speaks 126, 148
Applied Behavior/Applied Behavior Analysis
    (ABA) 7–8, 72–77

Behavioral/Emotional (domains) 5, 17, 20
Behaviorist (ism) 6,
Behavior Plan 20, 70, 75, 81, 82
Behavior Therapist 20
Boardmaker 9, 45–46, 78–79, 83

Central Coherence (Central
    Coherence Theory/Weak Central
    Coherence) 57–58
Childhood Disintegrative Disorder 2–3
Communication 2–5, 8, 10, 12, 16–18,
    20–23, 27–29, 31–50, 54–55, 64, 70,
    73, 74, 76–81, 84–87, 89–92, 120–125,
    134–135, 137, 143–145, 151–152,
    154–156, 158
Cognition 5, 20, 33, 52–55, 57, 59, 61,
    63–65, 67, 72, 81, 89
Cognitive Coaching 11–12

Developmental Individual Difference
    Relationship Model 9
Discrete Trial Training 7, 72

Early Intervention 5,
Echolalia 35–36, 39, 93,
Executive Function 59, 67,
Expressive language 20, 40–42, 46
Eye Gaze (contact) 32–33, 35, 37–38,
    42, 89, 91, 100

Floortime Model 10
Free Appropriate Public Education (FAPE) 23

Genetics 4
Greenspan, Stanley 10

Hypersensitivity 103
Hyposensitivity 103

Interventions (and treatment Models) 6, 9,
    35, 95,
    Behavioral 70, 85,
Impulse Control 22, 48, 59–60, 81
Individualized Education Program (IEP)/
    IEP Meetings 5, 23

Joint attention 37, 44, 63, 89–92

Kanner, Leo 1

Label-Free 25, 70, 100, 105, 112, 145
Learning Environment 123
Least Restrictive Environment (LRE) 16,
    24, 126, 146
Lovas, Ivar 8

Medical Challenges (and Behavior) 84
Modeling 64, 88, 94, 98, 110
Musical cognition 65
Musical perception 65
Music therapist (therapy) 5, 20, 25, 64, 136

Occupational therapist 5, 20, 105–106, 108,
    110, 112
One-on-one Support 124

Paraprofessional 22, 24, 26, 32, 47, 55, 64,
    70, 79, 92–93, 105- 106, 109, 112, 119,
    124–125, 127, 132–134, 143, 145

Peer interaction/contact 17–18, 26–28,
      33, 35, 37, 39, 54, 63, 65, 66, 71, 76,
      84, 87–89, 91–93, 95–100, 104, 118,
      128, 132
Pervasive Development Disorder 2
Physical Challenges (and Autism) 16, 46,
      105, 113, 123, 125, 137
Physical therapist 20, 110
Picture Exchange Communication System
      (PECS) 8, 36, 45
Proprioceptive Challenges 103–104, 106

Receptive language 34, 40, 43, 77, 109
Reciprocation 38, 43–45, 90–91, 134
Rett syndrome 2, 152–155
Reverse Inclusion 25, 99

Section 504 16
Self-efficacy 97
Self-stimulation 34, 75, 77, 111
Sensory needs (sensory breaks, sensory
      challenges) 16–17, 20–21, 34, 40–41,
      48, 54, 80, 103–113
Sensory dysfunction 103, 105, 107–109,
      111, 113
Sensory integration 103, 105
Sensory motor challenges 103–105,
      110, 112
Service Provider(s) 24, 72, 112
Shifting Set 60
Sign language 7, 26–27, 39, 47

Socialization (Social Skills, social
      development) 2–3, 6, 8, 10–12,
      16–19, 23, 25, 27, 31, 33, 39, 49, 53,
      63–64, 66, 70–71, 75, 83–84, 87–100,
      119, 121, 123, 125, 128, 135–138,
      141–144
Social Intelligence 55
Social Story (ies) 12, 48- 50, 56, 58, 79–80
Social worker 6, 19
Special education (including special
      education professionals) 5–7, 9–10,
      13, 16–21, 24, 26–27, 34–36, 39,
      44–46, 48, 50, 70–72, 75, 80–82, 84,
      90, 107, 109, 112, 113, 115, 117–119,
      121–124, 127, 132, 136, 144
Speech pathologists/therapist 5, 20
Spectrum disorder 2, 5
Student Profile(s) 17, 26

TEACCH (Treatment and Education
      of Autistic and Related
      Communication- Children Curriculum
      Handicapped) 8–9
Tactile Dysfunction 105, 107
Theory of mind 33, 55, 73

Verbal Behavior Analysis (VBA) 8
Vestibular challenges 104–107
Visual Dysfunction 108

Working Memory 59–60